An English Madam

The Life and Work of
Cynthia Payne

PAUL BAILEY

An English Madam

The Life and Work of
Cynthia Payne

JONATHAN CAPE
THIRTY BEDFORD SQUARE LONDON

First published 1982
Copyright © 1982 by Cynthia Payne and Paul Bailey
Jonathan Cape Ltd, 30 Bedford Square, London WC1

British Library Cataloguing in Publication Data
Bailey, Paul
 An English madam.
 1. Payne, Cynthia 2. Prostitutes—Biography
 I. Title
 338.7'6136344'0924   HQ117
 ISBN 0-224-02037-4

Acknowledgments

I wish to thank Keith Parker for much diligent research.

P.B.

The author and publishers would like to thank the *Spectator* for permission to quote the extract which appears on pp. 160–2, and also the following for permission to reproduce photographs: Associated Newspapers Ltd, 17; London Express News and Feature Services, 12, 15, 16, 18, 19; *Sunday People/Syndication International*, 7. All other photographs are from Cynthia Payne's own collection.

Printed in Great Britain by
Butler & Tanner Ltd, Frome and London

In Memoriam
Squadron Leader Robert (known as 'Mitchell') Smith
1906–1981

Contents

Illustrations

Preface

I first learned about Cynthia Payne and her extraordinary brothel one dismal afternoon in the reading room of a university library in Fargo, North Dakota. I remember laughing immoderately – to the astonishment of the other readers – at the account in an English newspaper of the raid on her disorderly house in the unlikely setting of Streatham. It was the Dickensian aspect of the story that appealed to me – the elderly clients clutching their 'luncheon vouchers'; the madam herself, who sounded like a kinder, if no less astute, Mrs Todgers. Even as I laughed, I experienced a curious feeling of national pride.

Now that I have heard that story from Cynthia, her 'girls', her clients, her slaves, as well as her relatives and friends, I can vouch for its authenticity. Everything in this book is true, though I have changed most of the participants' names and many of the locations. I am grateful to the customers particularly, for the frankness with which they discussed what D. H. Lawrence would have called their 'dirty little secrets'. Slave Philip, Slave Rodney, Gregory, Janet and Agatha all spoke with refreshing candour, as did the women who satisfied the not always ordinary needs of the middle-aged and elderly men whom Cynthia once catered for.

I can never thank Cynthia sufficiently for choosing me as her biographer. For one thing, there was the pleasure of her company – her observation that Prince Charles and his father spend a lot of time playing 'polio' seriously disrupted a day's work, I am happy to recall. I hope I have done justice to her unique way with words, since she is a compelling raconteuse, despite her limited vocabulary. This book is the expression of my affection and admiration for an extraordinary human being.

1982   P. B.

PROLOGUE

'A friend in Bangkok'

At ten minutes past four on the afternoon of Wednesday December 6th, 1978, a Christmas party of an unusual nature was brought to a close by Chief Superintendent Reginald Searles of the Streatham division of the Metropolitan Police.

The party, which had begun some three hours earlier, was being held at a large, detached, Victorian house in south-west London, situated next to a hall in which Emmeline Pankhurst lectured on women's suffrage in the early years of the century. The festivities were at their liveliest when the chief superintendent, his second-in-command, a sergeant and several constables of both sexes invaded the premises: those guests who were not actually engaged in sexual intercourse were either lining the staircase leading to the upper rooms in various states of anticipatory undress or relaxing over a post-coital drink in the capacious ground-floor lounge. One elderly reveller was discovered in the kitchen, restoring his depleted energy with the *specialité de la maison* – poached eggs on generously buttered toast.

The Streatham police had received an anonymous letter during the autumn, which insinuated that the residence in Ambleside Avenue was being used as a brothel. As a result, they had kept the premises under surveillance since September 15th. Three young constables and a sergeant had taken it in turns to watch and record each and every arrival and departure, even confiding to their notebooks the precise time the milkman deposited the customary pint on the doorstep and the postman delivered the mail. The diligent officers observed 249 men and fifty women enter the house, known as 'Cranmore', in the ten weeks prior to the party. One memorable morning, they had sighted a 'female type' of a notably masculine disposition bringing out the refuse.

The police were especially interested in the contents of the dustbins, much to the amusement of the householder, Cynthia Payne, who watched their determined scouring from her bedroom window. While they were appropriating used tissues and discarded letters, the evidence they were seeking was being consigned to an incinerator in the basement. Cynthia Payne's resourceful stoker ensured that the smell of burning rubber never drifted in the constables' direction.

The persevering policemen informed the chief superintendent that the bins were regularly filled with an extraordinarily large quantity of bottles and beer cans – enough to suggest that a well-stocked bar was in constant operation. Searles and his associates decided they had good reason to suspect that the owner of Cranmore was selling liquor without a licence, and secured a warrant enabling them to act on their suspicion – they would only pounce, though, when they felt confident that other, more serious charges could be levelled at the much-visited proprietor. Their confidence rose on December 6th, after fifty-three men and thirteen women were seen entering the house. The inequality of the numbers convinced them that the gathering had been assembled to do something more than celebrate the season.

Shortly after four o'clock, the sergeant and one of the constables walked up to the front door, and the sergeant rang the bell.

'I could hear the sound of voices and music,' stated the constable. 'I saw a movement through the glass in the door of someone wearing green. A voice that I now know to be that of Miss Payne said, "Who is it?" The sergeant said, "I am a police officer. I have a warrant to enter these premises. Open up." The door had started to open, but it was on a security chain and was then slammed shut. Together, the sergeant and I forced the door open by using our shoulders. As I entered the hall, I saw a coloured woman who was completely naked running down the stairs. She turned and pushed her way back up the stairs, through a number of men who were forming a queue.'

The next sight that greeted him was of another woman – clad only in red bra and panties – rushing out of the lounge. She stopped, registered the fact that the hall was filling up with police, and rushed back again. In what Cynthia Payne has designated the Group Sex Room, the constable saw a naked couple rising from a copious double bed – the man scurrying into his trousers, the woman clutching her underclothes.

Meanwhile, the sergeant – followed by a superintendent and several constables – made his way past the scantily dressed clerics, barristers and businessmen on the staircase, with a view to finding out what was going on in the upper rooms. Three more locks had to be broken. In the Mirror Room, which was reserved for people who enjoyed watching themselves perform, a dedicated pair were surprised in what looked like the full throes of passion.

They were ordered to stop whatever it was they were doing.

'Not until I've come,' said the man, who – an alert woman constable noticed – had neglected to remove his socks.

They were then ordered to stay where they were.

Boxes of tissues, packets of contraceptives, bottles of baby oil and tins of cream (Cynthia Payne considers Crowe's Cremine, the theatrical make-up remover, a perfect lubricant) were placed beside every bed; some lengths of rope and a variety of leather straps ('For the kinky bondage fellows') were in a plastic bag in the downstairs bathroom, and there were whips in the bedroom cupboards. A lone vibrator was held up for inspection by a curious constable. 'And what is this?' he asked Cynthia Payne, who replied, 'You're a man. You know what it is.' He shook his head. She told him what it was. Another constable discovered a box filled with vouchers to the values of 10p and 15p. 'What are these?' he asked her. 'They', she

3

answered, 'are my luncheon vouchers.' The policeman looked astonished. 'They are for my gentlemen to satisfy their appetites.'

Films with titles like *Hot Pussies* and *Der Landficker* were in a black shopping bag in the larder; *Bizarre Tastes*, *Naughty Girl Guides* and *Secret Spanking Cult* were among those hidden in a suitcase; a further five had been hastily deposited in the garden, while a Bisto tin in the kitchen was large enough to accommodate no less than nine, including the comparatively esoteric *The Way to Valhalla* and *Casanova and the Nuns*.

These, and similar, items were the kind of things the officer from the Obscene Publications Department of New Scotland Yard had expected to find. What intrigued him, and indeed all the other officers present, were the little slips of paper that appeared to have been distributed to the majority of the male guests. Why should such obviously successful men be in possession of the type of voucher similar to those their employees would use in cafés and pubs as part payment for lunch? Why were some of these men – who were absented from their jackets and trousers, and consequently their wallets and cheque books – carrying a token for this minuscule amount?

An Indian gentleman told the police that the voucher entitled him 'to have a sex affair'. Not all the partygoers were as honest: one supposed that it could be exchanged for his hat and coat when the time came to leave; another that it allowed him 'to see the pictures'; yet another thought it was a raffle ticket for a prize, and certainly not for sex – 'I'm a bit past it now'; many said that it was for food and drink, and even more remarked that they 'had no idea' what possible use it could be put to.

The police inquiries revealed that nearly all the male guests had paid Cynthia Payne £25 on entering Cranmore. This sum guaranteed them as much food and drink as they required, a film show, a lesbian display, and the services of a girl of their choice – but with the proviso that the girl herself was happy to oblige. One of the older clients explained why he was charged less: 'I only pay £15 because I don't go with a girl because I'm impotent.'

4

On receipt of the entrance fee, Cynthia Payne had handed over a 'luncheon voucher' which, in turn, was passed on to the customer's chosen woman. If a man wanted to 'go up-stairs' (the Payne euphemism for sexual intercourse) a second, third, or fourth time, then he would have to purchase a fresh voucher for each trip. At the end of an uninterrupted party, the obliging women would return the vouchers to Cynthia Payne and be given the appropriate payment for their work.

Just before the arrival of the police, the merry-makers had been shown a film and had witnessed two girls writhing on the floor of the lounge in simulated ecstasy. But that was not all. They had been given additional, and unexpected, enter-tainment that afternoon, thanks to a distinguished theologian – an acknowledged authority on monophysitism – and his versatile girl friend. This brilliant man hadn't travelled to Streatham in order to lecture on the teachings of Jacobus Bardaeus, as the astonished audience who relished his every thrust in the passageways at Ambleside Avenue soon dis-covered. Outside the college, Kasper is a determined and tireless exhibitionist, who has found in Beryl the ideal part-ner. The little local difficulties that prevent most of us from gratifying our desires on a momentary whim are the very things that spur them on to their greatest gymnastic achieve-ments. Cramped conditions feed their united imagination: one summer evening, when Kasper's car was stuck in a jam at Hyde Park Corner, Beryl stimulated him orally while the occupants of the lower deck of a bus watched in fascinated amazement. People still talk of the performance the couple sustained against the wash basin in the upstairs bathroom at Cranmore, when he – in a more than usually abandoned gesture – almost wrenched the basin from the wall; they remember, too, what feats he did that day, when – with Beryl's unbridled assistance – he dazzled them as they waited on the staircase with a series of stunning twists and turns. The police were unlucky in their timing, for they burst in only minutes after Beryl and Kasper had brought their act to a literally breathtaking climax, eliciting spontaneous applause. The pair were already dressed – he in black underpants, she in a red brassiere with matching knickers – when Chief Superintendent Searles commanded his officers to enter the house.

As soon as she had recovered from the shock – 'Oh my God, you had to raid me today. Why today, oh my God?' – Cynthia Payne assumed complete responsibility for everything that had taken place. She advised her friends to stay calm and to be careful what they told their interrogators. Even so, at least two of the girls broke down under questioning, despite their employer's repeated assurance that she alone was culpable. Only one of the women faced the ordeal with total aplomb: her constantly reiterated 'No comment' succeeded in reducing her questioner to a state bordering on the murderous.

Each man was asked how he had been invited to the party. To judge by the replies, the hostess had seriously neglected her duty and forgotten to issue invitations. She had favoured, rather, the unconventional method of telling people she *didn't* want to attend to inform those she *did*. Thus it was that one client after another just happened to bump into an old chum or a casual acquaintance or – most frequently – a perfect stranger who just happened to know that on the following afternoon a lady called either Cindy or Judith would be presiding over a 'sex party' from 1.30 onwards. These necessarily brief encounters – the message conveyed *sotto voce* – were staged in a large assortment of saloon bars: one gets the impression that on the evening of Tuesday December 5th, 1978, there was scarcely a pub in the south of England which did not contain a whispering informer anxious to pass on the glad tidings about the forthcoming frolics. A 'paddy' working on the M11 at Cambridge was also possessed of the information, though he seems to have been isolated in his knowledge – exactly how he communicated with his contact has not been revealed.

A man who was nearly caught *in flagrante delicto* (he was sockless, but his bedmate wasn't) shared with the waylaid motorist the distinction of not having chanced upon a saloon bar intelligencer the night before. 'I heard about it from a friend in Bangkok,' he told a constable. (In the police statement, the capital city of Thailand appears as 'Bancock' – an error that strikes one as peculiarly apt under the circumstances.) The young officer then inquired of the naked recipient of good news from the Far East, who was standing next to a not quite naked coloured woman, if his voucher had entitled him to the services of a prostitute. 'You should know. You smashed in the door.' Had he, the policeman continued, indulged in sexual intercourse? 'Halfway.' Another customer answered the same question by confessing that he hadn't yet, but was on the point of doing so. 'You got here too soon,' he said sadly.

Very few of the middle-aged and elderly men who were transported by van to Streatham police station for further questioning could be accounted 'kinky bondage fellows'. It was a rule of Cranmore that those requiring humiliation should be catered for in private, in an atmosphere conducive to their uncommon needs: a party was no occasion for wounds, however tastefully inflicted. According to one of the girls, all that was on offer was 'straight sex or hand relief'. There was, in fact, a heavy demand for the latter, principally because of the advanced age of certain of the clientèle, for whom even the missionary position was difficult to maintain.

When she was charged at ten o'clock that evening with 'running a brothel and keeping a disorderly house', Cynthia Payne repeated her statement that she accepted complete responsibility.

At the station, the 'female type' who had been observed carrying out the garbage from Cranmore was identified as Robert ('Mitchell') Smith, a former squadron leader in the Royal Air Force.

PART ONE

Her Life

I

'The wrong parent died'

Cynthia Payne's father was at sea when the elder of his two
daughters was born on December 24th, 1932. From the
R.M.S. *Windsor Castle*, off Cape Town, Hamilton Payne
wrote to his wife, Betty, in England:

> Fri 30 Dec
>
> How is my Darling and her little Cinders to-day? You have
> both been in my thoughts a lot for the last two days. I wish
> I was home to kiss you both. I wonder what my baby is
> like, it seems so hard to think that I have a baby + yet not
> seen her, she is now six days old. She ought to have grown
> a bit by now didn't she Bie? I pictured you again last night
> cuddling her up to you, how I did wish I was home ...
>
> Well this is Sunday Jan 1st I drank the old year out with
> Jack last night otherwise it's very quiet.
> How is my Darling + her baby to-day, I hope you are
> well, I'm longing to hear from you, it should be a nice long
> letter as you have been convalence for eight days now. Give
> Cinders a kiss for me, it's one consolation to think when
> you get this I shall be only two weeks away. Well bye-bye
> my sweetest of all ...

Hamilton Payne saw little of his family during the following ten years. For most of that time he was working as a ladies' hairdresser on the South African Union-Castle ocean liners. He would appear in England every three months or so, bearing costly gifts for his wife and children, with whom he would stay for about a week. 'It was like a stranger coming into the home,' Cynthia recalls. 'I never really knew him.'

Their home was a terrace house in a fashionable resort on the south-east coast. It was small, poky even, but for Hamilton, who had been raised in a dingy back street, it was spacious and grand. He was proud of the fact that he had entered into marriage as a householder, able to provide his young wife with a place of her own.

Cynthia's younger sister, Melanie, was conceived during one of Hamilton's brief visits. The women are close in age – Melanie is Cynthia's junior by eighteen months – but markedly different in every other respect. Their dissimilarities were pronounced from early childhood: Cynthia was always loudly self-assertive; Melanie demure and reticent. While Melanie was at home playing contentedly with her dolls, Cynthia was roaming the streets with a gang of boys. Melanie observed, and observes, the social niceties, whereas Cynthia has little patience with them: 'I like to shock people. I like to wake people up.'

'She was jealous from the start,' Melanie told me. 'She cut my curls off because everyone said what lovely curls I had and what a beautiful baby, so snip, snip. She used to pinch my bottle. It's a shame, really – we have nothing in common. I've got friends who are sisters and they do the same sort of things together. They paint and sew and make clothes, as I do. It's just temperament, I suppose – there's only one thing in Cynthia's life and that's sex. But there only ever has been.'

Cynthia and Melanie are united, however, in their enduring love for their mother. They also share an inability to feel genuine affection for the stranger who fathered them. Cynthia remembers Betty Payne as a very gentle, placid woman, 'a soft touch'. 'She never wanted much out of life. She didn't want lots of money – as long as she had enough for her two kids she was happy.' She was indifferent, it seems, to the expensive clothes that Hamilton bought for her in America and South Africa. 'I brought her a fur coat home,' he told his elder daughter many years later. 'Most women would have loved a fur coat in the 1940s. Most women would have wanted to put on the coat and go out on the town and show it off, but no, not your mother. She was at the stove when I got it out of its box, cooking chips for you and Melanie. "Very nice," she said. "Thank you." She just put the coat down and carried on preparing your meal. Most women would have rushed upstairs into the bedroom and preened themselves in front of the mirror, but not my Bie. "Very nice. Thank you" – that's all she said.'

Betty Payne died of cancer of the throat in 1943, at the age of thirty-eight, only months after Hamilton had returned home for good. He was desolated. His daughters were both hurt and bewildered, for they had noticed nothing wrong with their carefree, undemanding mother, apart from the fact that she was occasionally short of breath. They had seldom heard her complain. With her death, a source of warmth vanished from Cynthia's life, and from Melanie's, too: the next few years in Father's company were to be cold ones indeed. The girls, who had grown accustomed to being kissed and hugged, found their claims for affection rebuffed: Daddy had his shop to run, and had no time for such indulgences. Neither could he afford to placate his discontented children with exotic gifts, as he had once done in his ocean liner days. He was a constant presence now, not some strange bringer of clothes and toys, who would vanish as suddenly as he had come.

Betty Payne's last months were spent in the flat above her husband's hairdressing salon. In order to acquire the business, which was situated in the very centre of the seaside town, Hamilton had had to sell the house in which she had raised the girls. 'She wasn't happy in the flat. It didn't seem like a home to her. She missed her garden.' Hamilton had assured her that she would have a bigger and better house when he had really established himself, and she had accepted his assurance. At the start, he couldn't afford to employ an assistant, which meant that she was required to help him in the shop. She was working alongside him only a week before her death. She had confided in one or two close relatives that she 'felt bad', but had told no one else, not even her husband, how ill she was. It was only when she began to feel worse, when she was quite literally in agony, that she allowed herself to be taken to hospital.

Hamilton's grief was exacerbated by the fact that he had seen so little of his wife during the dozen years of their marriage. When it was no longer possible to work on the ocean liners, he had joined the Merchant Navy and his visits home had been rarer and briefer. Now, when he was at last demobilized, and free to enjoy being a husband and father, the woman he loved was cruelly taken from him. 'She had to die to make him more humble. He might have been more arrogant than he was if she'd gone on living.'

For Hamilton Payne was not a modest man, as his daughters remember sadly. The youngest of five children, he had risen from working-class origins and attained what he considered respectable status. On the liners, he had cut and set the hair of the wealthy and famous, and had been changed by the experience. He had been a nobody when he had first left England; when he came back for good it was as someone who could boast that his work had met with the delighted approval of Gracie Fields, among others. He was, he maintained to his children, a pillar of sorts in the local community. He was his own man, a professional, and he expected people – particularly Cynthia and Melanie – to look up to him.

Melanie was the ideal daughter – on the surface, at least – for such a man. Even at the age of nine, she was behaving in a distinctly ladylike way. Although she was a chatterbox like her sister, her voice was appropriately measured and her vocabulary comparatively sophisticated. She was always neatly dressed. Cynthia, who had been permitted by her mother to run loose, was commanded by Hamilton to emulate her sister in speech and appearance. 'I was a problem child. I was a proper little bugger, you know. I used to go with the boys from the housing estate. My sister thought they were common. I didn't have sex, nothing like that, but I loved being with boys, never with girls.' The boys were working-class, and the ambitious, snobbish Hamilton was horrified that Cynthia was harming his reputation in the town by playing with them. She was, in fact, the leader of the gang: its driving force, its most inventive rebel. 'The kids Dad considered decent were warned by their mothers to stay away from me.'

Her father assumed the role of martinet. The more he tried to discipline her, though, the more she crossed him. He cautioned her frequently about her obsessive, as well as excessive, use of swear words. Years earlier, he had beaten her, when – in the Anderson shelter behind the house – she had whispered to Melanie, with whom she was sharing a bunk, that their parents were getting undressed. 'Let's take a look and see if we can see Daddy's cock,' was the sentence that precipitated the beating. 'He pulled me out of the shelter and gave me a bloody good hiding on the backside. My mother, who was always trying to protect me, said, "It's nothing, Hamilton. Don't hurt her." "It's *nothing*," he said, "a girl of eight talking that kind of dirty talk? It's *nothing*!"'

After recounting that episode, Cynthia observed, 'I was just curious.' And then she asked, 'Should a girl of eight be interested in knowing what her Daddy's cock looks like?'

The first school that Cynthia Payne attended was a private one called, inexplicably, 'Dunheved'. Her report for the term ending at Easter, 1938, bears the information that her conduct is 'excellent', that she is 'making very good progress in English', that her 'counting and tables are coming on nicely', that her hand work is 'very good', and that she has 'a good ear' for singing. In the art class, the paragon is 'very observant and has a good memory'.

Despite this high praise, Hamilton took her out of 'Dunheved' when she was seven and placed her in another private school, where she did not do so well. From there she went on to a convent school, 'Villa Maddalena', from which she was expelled after pulling off a nun's veil and pinning a notice on a teacher's back. The principal, Sister Flavia, went to Hamilton's shop and told him that Cynthia would have to be removed. 'Is it because of her dirty talk?' he asked the nun, who replied that it wasn't: the expulsion was necessary because of the effect her waywardness was having on the other pupils. Cynthia's sole interest was in making mischief.

'When my mother died, I found it difficult to learn': by the time Cynthia was accepted at a council school, her regress as a student was complete. She was joined there by her resentful sister, who was taken out of 'Villa Maddalena' by an angry Hamilton, who decided he would spend no more money on his daughters' education. Melanie did her best to dissociate herself from Cynthia, who had immediately befriended what Melanie calls 'the riff-raff'.

Cynthia's cousin, Winifred – an amiable, tolerant woman, who regards her unconventional relative with bemused admiration – cannot remember a time when Cynthia wasn't talking about sex. 'She was a monkey. She always knew more than anybody else. I was older, but she told me the facts of life.' These 'facts', it transpired, were sometimes wildly inaccurate, the product of an imagination that dwelt continually on the erotic delights awaiting its owner. While her classmates were studying their textbooks, Cynthia was directing her attention to the stories in teenage magazines like the *Oracle* and *Miracle*. They confused and excited her. The confusion arose from what she detected was a missing element. The hero of the average story would take the beautiful young heroine in his arms and 'crush' his lips against hers. The result of this crushing would become noticeable several months later when the heroine would joyfully inform her hero, 'Darling, I'm going to have your baby!' How, Cynthia wondered, could a pair of crushing lips produce a child? There was more to conception than that, and she set her mind to discovering what it was. It was the vocal expression she gave this perfectly natural curiosity that embarrassed and offended most of her adult relations, who responded to her frank questioning with disgusted references to 'dirty talk'. No one, it appears, made the attempt to explain – in words that have not been debased – how a man impregnates a woman. Rather than tell her that the parts of the body have proper names, they replied with confident predictions that

16

she would 'go to the bad'. Even her beloved Aunt Maud, who treated her fondly, announced that Cynthia would give birth to an illegitimate child by the time she was fourteen.

Maud was wrong, and Cynthia did not 'go to the bad' as surely and swiftly as her family predicted. She continued to swear, though, because this was her 'natural way of speaking'. She was still the ringleader of the gang, in defiance of Hamilton's wishes – she even took to stealing her father's cigarettes to give to her mates, who had started smoking. The boys, from whom she had learned her 'dirty talk', were under no compulsion to refer to their cocks as penes, or their balls as testicles: they were happily unaware, as indeed Cynthia was, of those precise alternatives. She granted them a glimpse of her fanny, not her vagina, and they returned the favour by undoing their trouser buttons. 'I showed them mine, and they showed me theirs. It was all very innocent. There was no thought of sex.' They were more interested in climbing trees or disturbing respectable children.

After his wife's death, Hamilton Payne employed a housekeeper to take charge of his daughters. She did not last long. In their different ways, Cynthia and Melanie made her life intolerable. They resented the intruder, who was obviously anxious to marry their father. They were briefly in accord in their antipathy.

Another housekeeper was hired. She, too, was forced to endure Melanie's decorous insults and Cynthia's outspokenness. Like her predecessor, she was hunting for a husband – or so the girls assumed. She also left when the situation became unbearable.

A third was engaged. She was afforded the same treatment. She departed in haste. Hamilton, exasperated by their behaviour, made it clear to Melanie and Cynthia that, young as they were, they would now have to fend for themselves.

And that is what they did, after a fashion. Melanie played the role of Hamilton's ideal daughter so well that her father almost forgot that this was the girl who had cajoled Betty into letting her stay with her godmother whenever he was home from sea. In the decade or so that she lived above the salon,Melanie seldom revealed the keen dislike she still harboured for Hamilton, which she had expressed as a child by disappearing from him: 'When she knew he was due back, she would make arrangements to go off to Littlehampton. She couldn't bear him.' During those years in which there was no possibility of escape, she acted with calculated politeness. She rarely argued with the frequently unreasonable Hamilton – she merely acknowledged that he was right, even when he patently wasn't. Melanie was as compliant as her sister was belligerent: 'She took the line of least resistance, whereas I always stood up to him.'

Hamilton was particularly annoyed by Cynthia's indifference to doing housework, an indifference she was pleased to have inherited from her mother: 'Mum would give the house a quick dust-over the day before Dad was expected home. He'd kick up a terrible fuss if he saw so much as a speck.' These days, Cynthia has a retinue of slaves to keep Cranmore neat and tidy. She stands behind Philip with a whip as he scrubs and polishes, and flays his naked flesh if he slackens at his appointed task; she commands the contentedly servile Rodney to mow the lawn and sweep the drive, and shrieks at those menials who are honoured with bathroom duties: 'Wash that scum off, slave!' and 'Too high and mighty for the S-bend, are you? We'll soon see about that!' But in the late 1940s, Cynthia was required to do all those chores she now relegates to her underlings. Hamilton, who considered it natural for a girl to be house proud, could not understand his firstborn's disinclination to set to it with a mop or pick up a duster. Cynthia remembers one occasion when she drove him into a fury. Instead of washing the dishes as she had been instructed, she had stacked them up inside the stove. It was her intention to deal with them the following morning. Hamilton, returning to the flat in the small hours, noticed that the plates were missing. He pulled Cynthia out of bed, and demanded to know where they were. After much prevaricating, she told him. He frog-marched her into the kitchen, where he stood over her while she washed up. 'I kept saying, "I'll do them tomorrow, I'll do them tomorrow."

"You'll bloody well do them tonight," he said. And I bloody well had to.'

It is one of the oddities of Hamilton's character that he encouraged neither Cynthia nor Melanie to learn how to cook. 'We ate out almost every night. It was cheaper, Dad reckoned, than buying meat and vegetables and preparing them at home.' Only on Sundays, when they visited either pair of grandparents, did they sit down to what Cynthia calls 'proper food' in a family atmosphere: 'We used to live for the weekends.' It was on such visits that Cynthia would inform Winifred of her latest findings in the sexual sphere.

To please her father, Cynthia agreed to study to become a qualified hairdresser. He enrolled her at a technical school in the West End of London. Hamilton at last felt confident that his rebellious child would have a vocation, a purpose in life – and one, moreover, that might prove beneficial to him. He urged her to take her training seriously, to apply herself. She promised him that she would do her best.

It was a promise she was unable to fulfil – at least, to his satisfaction. She found that she couldn't concentrate. Although she took the seven o'clock train to the capital every morning, she arrived at the college later and later. The city held too many distractions for her, of the kind an unsettled girl from a small town had difficulty resisting: she stared longingly into the windows of the big department stores, and stopped to admire the well-dressed women who passed her in the streets. And, at the forefront of her mind, there was the yet-to-be encountered lover – a Londoner, perhaps – who would crush his lips against hers. She awaited him eagerly.

Her lips remained uncrushed, though, and her propensity for day-dreaming became more and more noticeable. Her school work, such as it was, deteriorated. On July 21st, 1948, Hamilton Payne received a letter from the principal of the college – a somewhat confused woman, as her communication demonstrates:

I feel I must write and tell you that Sylvia is proving very slow in the uptake and is so far below the average student that we feel that it is a waste of her time and ours for her to continue the training.

We are sorry to come to this conclusion as you are in the trade and Sylvia has to make such a long journey to get the instruction, but we feel that she shows no sign whatever of any likelihood of reaching the prescribed standard for the School Certificate by the end of the training. You may, therefore, like to withdraw her at the end of the term.

Please do not blame Sylvia as she has given no trouble and is apparently doing her best.

In his hastily despatched reply to the principal, Hamilton no doubt observed that the subject of her anxiety was called Cynthia. No apology is offered in her next letter, dated July 23rd, which begins, 'We are all very concerned about Cynthia' and continues:

She does not seem to grasp the importance of her training. If you wish, we are quite prepared to give her another term in which to mend her ways.

Let me give you an instance. As you know, she is losing at least an hour a day on account of her late arrival and early departure. Instead of appreciating that extra effort is necessary to make up for this lost time, she arrived one day about 10 o'clock and told her mistress that she did not feel like hurrying, she had just dawdled.

She was sent with a register the other day to another part of the building and she was absent over half an hour and was found wandering about taking no active steps to find where the register was to be deposited.

Perhaps you would have a good talk to her and impress upon her that concentration and real interest are necessary.

His talk made no impression. He withdrew her from the school.

Every morning during her year as a trainee hairdresser, Cynthia had been given two shillings and sixpence by Hamilton

20

to pay for lunch. She saved the money instead, and when she had accumulated enough she went to C & A Modes in Oxford Street and spent it on clothes. 'You could buy a really lovely dress for a pound in those days.'

She had something, therefore, to show for her time in London – a substantially larger wardrobe. She was nearly sixteen and had vague aspirations about becoming a film star: 'I didn't want to live the restricted life of a girl from a good family.' What she wanted, desperately, was to leave home. She felt constrained there – by her father's censoriousness, by her sister's disapproval.

Cynthia was delighted when Hamilton told her that he had arranged for her to work for some friends of his in Aldershot. Felicity and Felix were prepared to teach her everything she had failed to learn at the college, and would pay her besides. They also assured Hamilton – though he did not reveal this to his daughter – that they would make the attempt to exercise some control over her and see that she behaved herself. This assurance was the source of his own delight when Cynthia departed.

She was happy at first. Felix had a thriving business and employed several assistants, all of them two or three years older than Cynthia. She revelled in their company, and they in hers. She listened, enraptured, as they talked about their boyfriends. She questioned them incessantly, to their considerable amusement. She pestered them for intimate details.

Felicity was more alarmed than amused. The mother of two small children, she was outraged by the coarseness of Cynthia's language. She wrote to Hamilton to that effect. Was Cynthia's compulsive swearing, she wondered, the result of some mental disturbance, occasioned by the sudden death of her mother? If so, did he not think it right that she should be examined by a psychiatrist?

Hamilton didn't think it was right. Whatever was wrong with Cinders, he reasoned, it wasn't *that*. She was going through a difficult phase, nothing more.

Felicity persisted. It *was* something more. The fact that Cynthia hadn't heeded a single one of the hundreds of warnings she'd received from her family, from her teachers, and

– most important – from her present employers, was proof enough.

'She thought there was something wrong with me. She had the cheek to send me to Park Prewett, the mental hospital in Basingstoke. My father was a bit annoyed because he had to pay for the treatment. Oh, it was a bloody horrible place – everyone looking at you as if you was crazy. I didn't know it was a loony bin when she first mentioned that I ought to go there. I thought to myself, "It'll make a nice day out." I only went to get out of the shop for a day.'

Cynthia's strongest memory of the psychiatrist who tried in vain to treat her at Park Prewett is that he smoked du Maurier cigarettes – a most exclusive brand in the 1940s. Even her father, with his 'posh' ambitions, didn't rise to those.

'He paced up and down in front of me, smoking a du Maurier cigarette. I'll never forget it. He said, "I want you to tell me all the dirty words you know beginning with 'A'." She must have briefed him. I must have said "arse", or "arsehole", or something. We got to "B". I suppose I said "bastard", "bloody". "Think of all the filthy dirty words," he kept on saying. I just didn't like him. I had the feeling he was getting all sexed-up, the way he was carrying on. He got to "C". I don't know whether I said "cunt", I can't remember. I'm sure I didn't. Then all of a sudden, we were at the letter "F". Now, I was all right until we got to the letter "F". "Do you know any word beginning with 'F'?" I said no. He said, "Surely you must know a word starting with 'F'?" I said, "I don't. I don't know one." And I'll never forget, he was sucking his du Maurier cigarette and pacing up and down ... I mean, he was really annoyed. Then he stopped and said to me, "How do you expect me to help you if you're not prepared to help yourself?" So I turned round and I said, "I don't want you to help me. I'm not here of my own free will. I don't want you to help me!" He looked at me; he was speechless. I wouldn't tell him the word "fuck" – that's what he wanted to hear. I was determined I wasn't going to say "fuck".'

She visited the hospital four more times. The psychiatrist

1, 2 and 3. Dressing up was Cynthia's favourite game.

4. Cynthia, aged nine.

5. Aged seventeen, with Keith.

6. Cynthia in her first house with one of her dogs, about 1970.

wrote to Hamilton that 'something had happened in Cynthia's adolescence', but he couldn't ascertain what.

'My father got fed up with having to pay. He said to Felicity he didn't agree with her sending me up there. He didn't think it could be that bad, otherwise the psychiatrist would have said so. She was furious, Felicity was. She always thought the worst of me.'

It was while she was living with Felix and Felicity that Cynthia met Keith, with whom she had her first, rudimentary sexual experience.

'I'd been going out with him for two or three weeks and nothing had happened. If he'd been more forceful, we might have done something. I'd have let him. We went to see a film with Betty Hutton – I remember it because of the song "It Had To Be You". I was sitting up in the gods with Keith's arm round me – he was a shy bloke, it took him bloody eternity to get his arm round me. Anyway, the next thing was, his hand was on my bust. He was feeling my tits and I just burst out crying. I suppose I was emotional, I don't know. I do know I thought, "Oooh, I like that. I really like that" – but I was a bit ashamed for liking it so much. It was a very odd feeling – I'd talked about sex, all that dirty talk, on and on and on, yet when it happened I shed tears. I cried and cried. He asked me what was wrong, and I said I didn't know. Then he stopped what he was doing.'

They went out together for several weeks. The prospect of tears deterred Keith from making further overtures. Cynthia ached with frustration – as did Keith, presumably – but was unable to take his hands and put them where she wanted them. It was up to the man to make the first move. 'We've laughed about it since. "Christ," he said, "I didn't want to start you sobbing all over again."'

Out of sheer devilment, perhaps, Cynthia staged a scene inspired by her copious reading of the *Oracle*. She used Doris, the nursemaid to Felicity and Felix's children, as her startled informant. She managed to get Doris alone: 'I've something to tell you,' she whispered conspiratorially. She made her features appropriately distraught before she announced that she was going to have a baby. 'I love him so very, very much. I want to have his child. Oh, Doris, Doris, please understand, Doris, that I would travel to the ends of the earth for him. I would suffer any shame just so long as I could keep his love!'

The gullible Doris was moved by Cynthia's outpourings. She promised to help the unfortunate girl. She advised her to calm down. The boy might turn out to be responsible – the idea of being a father often brought thoughtless young men to their senses. All would be for the best, in the long run.

'I hope so, Doris. My heart yearns for him. I don't think I could go on living if he deserted me now!'

Cynthia was so carried away by her own acting powers that she forgot to tell Doris that the precious information she had imparted with such dramatic emphasis was for Doris's ears only. The necessary cliché – 'Let this be our secret' – did not come to her recently crushed lips.

Doris immediately told Felix's assistants that little Cindy was pregnant. They were instantly attentive to her. Like Doris, they promised help. They would rally round her if the boy let her down. She was not to worry. They hugged and kissed her and assured her of their genuine concern.

Cynthia's happiness – the happiness of being the object of sympathy and disinterested affection – was short-lived. The following day, she was called into Felicity's presence. Felicity never rose before ten in the morning and was in the habit of receiving people in her bedroom. 'You'd have thought she was the lady of the manor, the way she behaved. She put on airs something shocking.'

Felicity's reaction to the news Doris had passed on to her was entirely predictable.

'It comes as no surprise to me to learn that you are going to have a baby. I have known from when you were a child that you would end up this way.'

It wasn't until Felicity said, 'Cindy, I have no alternative but to send you back home,' that Cynthia terminated her performance and returned to reality. She spoke the truth. 'I'm not pregnant. I was play-acting. I was having a bit of fun.'

'I'm afraid I don't believe you.'

Spurred on by Felicity's disbelief, Cynthia stated – with a typical lack of finesse – that since she hadn't even been fucked, it was impossible for her to be having a baby. 'He was too shy to fuck me,' she elaborated, to Felicity's horror. 'He only felt my tits. That's all he did. All he did was feel my tits in the pictures.'

'Felix and I can't afford to wait and find out if you are being honest.'

She pleaded with Felicity not to send her back to her father. She begged her not to do that. She told the lady whose presence she had been called into that she really and truly had not been fucked.

She was ordered out of the bedroom.

'I was very, very unhappy. The last thing I wanted was to go home. I hated it there.'

In her distress, Cynthia decided that the only way she could make Felicity feel sorry for her was to pretend to commit suicide. She took a bottle of weed killer from the garden shed and wrote a farewell note – 'I was always dramatic' – to Felix and Felicity. In it, she declared that she was going to end it all in the downstairs bathroom by drinking poison. She would rather die than return to her father.

She placed the note in a prominent position in the hall and duly locked herself in the bathroom. She listened eagerly for Felix to come in from the salon. She heard him rush up the stairs, shouting to his wife, 'Where's Cindy? Is she with you? Have you seen Cindy?'

No, she hadn't seen her. Why on earth was he in such a panic?

Cynthia waited a moment or two before opening the bathroom door, upon which Felix was clamouring frantically.

'I'd gone to all that trouble, but I hadn't done anything. I hadn't even unscrewed the top of the bottle of weed killer. He was relieved to find me alive, but he was bloody angry too.'

She was called into the presence for the last time.

'Why did you think of killing yourself?'

'Because I don't want to go back to him.'

Felicity explained that suicide was a dreadful sin, a crime.

'We were all on put on this earth to do something. You must do what you are here to do until your proper span is ended. I am sorry, but I am still sending you home.'

And home she went, to a dismayed and disgusted Hamilton, who said that he was going to have her examined by a gynaecologist. 'We'll soon discover if you're telling lies.' She insisted that she was innocent. Her godmother, in whom she confided a few days later, believed her when she described what had, and hadn't, happened with Keith. 'I told her it was just for fun; it was just to shock.' There was no examination.

Cynthia's godmother, who was also Melanie's, had written to Hamilton three years earlier:

I think you will find Cindy will be O.K. when she grows a little older – of course she is at an awkward age now – she is a child one minute – grown up the next – a sort of mixture all the time. I think too she misses her mother – not outwardly but inwardly, which makes her feel at sixes and sevens with everything and everyone at times. I shouldn't worry, that will all pass. I agree she is a child that won't be driven but led and often to appeal to her better nature would work wonders.

'He lost interest in me. "You do what you want," he said.'

She had no idea what she wanted to do. 'I tried for his sake to be a hairdresser, but I wasn't any good. After all the training at the school and the months I spent working for Felix, I could just about manage a shampoo properly. I used to love talking to the customers and making them laugh. I used to enjoy that, talking to the customers and making them roll up.'

She had a succession of different jobs. Whether as shop assistant or waitress, her principal concern was in diverting the customers. She was unemployed for long periods. Her father accused her of being the one and only lazy member of the Payne family.

Hamilton did not appeal to Cynthia's better nature. He lost interest in his daughter's welfare to such an extent that he abnegated any claim to parental responsibility. He was simply concerned with his own good name when Cynthia embarked on the first of her disastrous relationships, with a man in his early forties. His efforts to extricate her from the liaison were of a crudely dictatorial kind. He allowed himself nothing more than the expression of outrage. He was incapable then, and for many years afterwards, of displaying any sign of tenderness to his children, who have remained in agreement that – to use Cynthia's phrase – 'the wrong parent died'.

2

'He only wanted sex'

Hamilton Payne drank heavily, but not in front of his children. Thanks to his large capacity for alcohol, he was able to walk a straight line back from the pub on Saturday nights.

Cynthia could tell when he was drunk, though. It was then that he became more than usually waspish, more than usually critical. Under the influence, he discerned new inadequacies in his elder daughter.

'He was only pleasant when there was a woman around': Cynthia's percipience on sexual matters has its origins in her early observations of her father's behaviour. She studied his moods, and noted that he was at his least dictatorial when he was seeing 'Jersey Lil' regularly. 'We called her that because she came from Jersey. She was very dark and very attractive, very Spanish-looking.' 'Jersey Lil' never slept at the flat, but Cynthia guessed eventually that she and Hamilton were lovers. 'I knew subconsciously that my Daddy was in a good mood because he'd been out with her.'

'Jersey Lil' wanted to marry Hamilton. 'I think they would have married, but Dad said it was Melanie's jealousy that stopped them. "Jersey Lil" was supposed to have said to him, "Cindy I can manage, Cindy is no problem – it's Melanie who bothers me."'

Melanie confessed to Cynthia at Hamilton's funeral in 1979 that she had deeply resented the attention he had paid to 'Jersey Lil'. She had seen 'Lil' hanging on her father's arm in the salon a mere three months after their mother's death. The sight had enraged her.

There was another 'Lil' in Hamilton's life: '"Diamond Lil" was aristocratic, a duchess-type of woman, big-busted.' She, too, had marriage in mind. Melanie approved of her. Unlike 'Jersey', 'Diamond' did not indulge in tasteless flirting. She treated the widower with a proper circumspection.

Hamilton might have married 'Diamond Lil' if she hadn't been wealthy. He needed to be admired for his prowess as a breadwinner. He took pride in the fact that his was a profitable business. It was imperative that he amass his own wealth. He did not want to be known in the town as 'Mr Morton': he feared that kind of sarcasm. 'Diamond Lil' Morton had to be transformed into doting Mrs Payne. While she was richer than he, that transformation was a pipe-dream.

'She wouldn't have worn the trousers. She was quite submissible. I think he was a fool. He should have married her. I met her in 1977 at a Freemasons' dinner – Dad was once a Worshipful Master; he'd lain it on specially – and she said to me, "You know, Cynthia, your father's the same to me now as when I first knew him twenty years ago." In other words, he hadn't had sex with her.'

He enjoyed seeing 'Jersey' and being seen with 'Diamond'. Many of his later troubles might well have been averted had he taken one of them as his wife, especially in the light of 'Jersey's' claim that she could 'manage' Cindy. She must have been the only person among the Paynes' acquaintances who didn't consider Cynthia a problem. A persuasive, loving stepmother – a surrogate Betty – would have been capable, as Hamilton wasn't, of deterring Terence.

Hamilton resisted both willing 'Lils'. And when neither was available to keep him company, he drank.

'I was so forthright I used to put boys off. I was so direct I scared them away. Most of the men I fancied were shy. We never even got started.'

Derek was not put off, or scared away. 'He wasn't backward

at coming forward. I'd say he was my first real man. I was ready for it, and he could see I was. He looked like a film star. Oh, he was bloody handsome.'

Derek, who was only a little older than Cynthia, lived with his grandmother, who often went off at weekends to stay with friends or relatives. It was on one such weekend that Derek suggested to Cynthia she should spend Saturday night with him. The prospect thrilled her. 'I said to my father, I don't know how I got the words out, "I'm not coming home to-night. I shall be staying at Pauline's" – I can't remember whose name I came up with; it was a girl he knew I knew, that I do recall – and you can imagine my relief when he didn't kick up a fuss. He just nodded. I could hardly believe my luck.'

Derek took Cynthia to the Rex ballroom. 'It was marvel-lous. Oh, he was gorgeous with his jet-black hair, really swish. As he led me round the floor, I kept thinking, "I'm going to lie in your arms tonight. I'm going to wake up beside you in the morning." And, of course, the fact that my father hadn't a clue what I was doing – that excited me too.'

They went back to Derek's grandmother's house, where he was careful to check that the old lady hadn't returned unex-pectedly. 'It was all new, me spending a night – a whole night – with a man. Oh, he was bloody vain – he took his time coming into the bedroom. He was sprucing himself up, you see, putting on extra after-shave, I suppose. When he came in, he was wearing yellow pyjamas – bright canary yellow pyjamas. He was doing all that for me. He stood at the foot of the bed and fixed me straight in the eye. It was the most exciting moment of my life.'

Derek made love to her – 'properly' – three or four times. 'I had a boy friend at last. "This is going to be serious," I told myself. I thought he was my ideal man.'

They were alarmed early on Sunday morning by a loud knocking at the front door.

'"Oh, my God, it's my uncle," he said. "I'll have to let him in." "Oh no," I said. I was terrified. "Get under the bed," he said. I did; it was a fourposter; I got right under. He handed me my clothes in a heap. Derek tried to act very casual when he heard his uncle let himself in: I don't know why his uncle bothered to knock because he had his own key to the house. He came up the stairs, shouting for Derek. He walked into the bedroom and said, "I understand you brought a girl home last night." Word spread through the town – it was that kind of place. (I could never have opened a brothel there. I would have been told to close it down within the hour.) "Me bring a girl home, Uncle Peter? Whatever gave you that idea?" He sounded ever so cool and collected, Derek did, from where I was. His uncle had this dog with him, and no sooner was it in the room than the bloody thing started sniffing round me. Sniff, sniff; yap, yap – I was scared the little sod was going to give me away. Derek was lying in bed in his yellow pyjamas, all natural-like, and there was I on the floor with this dog sniffing me one minute and barking at me the next. "You just behave yourself while your grand-mother's gone," Derek's uncle said. Then off he went with the dog, and not before bloody time.'

That memorable weekend saw the beginning and end of Cynthia's affair with Derek. It seems likely that Hamilton had a hand in terminating the relationship. The respected businessman probably commanded the youth to stop seeing his daughter. 'I think my father stopped a lot of boys who wanted to take me out. I was never allowed to grow up naturally.'

Cynthia was in brief employment with the Southdown Bus Company when she was introduced to Terence. Gary, who effected the introduction, was worried about her infatuation with Derek: Terence, he told her, would look after her prop-erly; you couldn't trust boys, especially handsome ones like Derek. They were in the business of breaking hearts.

'Gary was a kind bloke. I looked upon him as a father – I didn't know then, and neither did he, that he'd given me the wrong advice. I used to show him my legs and I'd say, "Don't I have lovely legs, eh, Gary?" and he'd go all red. Grown-up as he was, he was another of the shy ones. He could have had his way with me if he'd plucked up the courage. He introduced me to Terry instead.'

Cynthia showed her legs to others besides the blushing Gary. In the office above the bus station, she raised her skirt for drivers and conductors alike: 'Most of them were over forty. It gave them a thrill, me letting them have a glimpse of my knickers.' Her flow of 'dirty talk' was now unstoppable – except when she had to answer the telephone and advise Southdown's customers about connections and schedules. Her audience grew. The tiny office was crammed throughout the day with men who were curious to see and hear the cheeky seventeen-year-old who lifted her dress when the fit was on her: 'They all got hard-ons. Oh, I was a dreadful little tease.'

The upstairs entertainment was brought to a sudden end by the station manager, who had been informed by his secretary of the disgusting goings-on around the switchboard. 'She was responsible for me getting the sack. I was a bad influence, she said. The men weren't concentrating; they were behind with their work. It was true. I suppose I can't blame her, thinking back on it – some of them wouldn't leave the office until I'd given them a quick flash, and they had passengers waiting down below. If I'd stayed with the company, there would have been bloody pandemonium in the depot.'

Her long affair with Terence began in uneasy circumstances.

'He tried to get me drinking. Not drunk, just merry. Merry for Terry. "Get her drinking and I'll have my oats quicker" – young as I was, I could see that was how his mind was working. But he didn't need to make me drink. I was willing enough without booze inside me. Anyway, he never succeeded. I only ever had a few.'

An additional problem at the outset was that Hamilton insisted Cynthia was home and ready for bed by 10.30 at the latest.

'I *was* ready for bed, but not in the way my father imagined. By half-past ten, I was wanting sex. I wasn't going to let that bloody tyrant stop me. So I hit on a brainwave. There was a small garden behind the premises, with its own gate which you could enter from a back street. You know what they say, where there's a garden there's bound to be a shed – well, we did have a shed, filled up with junk. My father was no gardener – he seldom went into it. I started to come home at ten. I would kiss Dad goodnight, and perhaps I'd yawn a bit before going to my room. He didn't suspect a thing, I was that bloody crafty. I'd wait for him to go to sleep, and when I heard him snoring I'd creep down the stairs and open the garden gate for Terry. Oh, it was exciting – eleven o'clock, midnight, having a lover waiting outside, panting for me. I'd already put some blankets and pillows in the shed; I'd sneaked them out one afternoon while Dad was busy in the shop. I made it nice and cosy in there. I've always liked my luxury – a fuck on the bare floorboards didn't appeal to me, to be honest, even at that age. It looked as near to a boudoir as I could make it. I've had nooky in more comfortable places, but oh, we had some bloody wonderful nights in that shed!'

On one of those nights, a night that began 'bloody wonderfully', Terry, in his haste to join Cynthia, forgot to lock the gate behind him.

'We had this broken paving-stone in the garden. All of a sudden, I heard someone tread on it. You know, it made a definite noise. Terry and I had just finished. I must have almost ruptured him, the way I shot up. "Oh God, Terry, he's suspected," I said. "He'll kill me if he catches us." The footsteps were coming nearer and I was shaking with fright. The next thing was, the door was flung open and a bloody great big torch was shining on us. I was still thinking it was my father – I mean, I couldn't look, I was so scared. There was Terry with his trousers down and me with my nightie off – you would have had to have been retarded not to know what we'd been doing. Then this voice said, ever so polite it was, "I beg your pardon, Madam." It was a policeman. He'd been checking all the business properties, front and back, and he'd noticed that the garden gate was open. I remember looking up at him and saying, "Thank God you're not my father." Those were my very words. I think I said it more than once, out of sheer relief. The copper apologized and went out, and

33

we made bloody sure that gate was always locked from that night on.'

There were consequences, to her respectable sister's discredit. 'Word got round at the police station that Hamilton Payne's daughter had been caught having a bunk-up in the garden shed. I don't think my father heard about it. But a few years later, when Melanie announced her engagement to Kevin, a policeman, who was attached to the same station, the subject came up again. He was ribbed about it. The younger coppers asked him if Melanie was as much fun in the shed as Cindy – by that time, I had a really terrible name in the town. He wasn't amused. In fact, he was bloody furious. He said it made things look bad for my sister. Some of the policemen actually thought he was marrying *me*. That made him even more hot under the collar.'

'He stood up to my father. I loved a man who could do that.'

Terence was only slightly younger than Hamilton, and therefore couldn't be warned off as Derek had been. '"I'm going to take Cynthia out tonight whether you like it or not" – that's the way he spoke to him. "Don't be stupid, Hamilton" – oh, it was bloody music to my ears, hearing him say, "Don't be stupid, Hamilton." Terry wasn't handsome like Derek was. He wouldn't have looked anything special in canary yellow pyjamas. He had a personality, though. He was fairly dominating, which I liked, but he wasn't a bully.'

Hamilton hated Terence, and his feelings were reciprocated. Cynthia, not surprisingly, sided with her lover. Such was the gulf between father and daughter that she dismissed Hamilton's reasonable – for once – misgivings as obstreperousness. He doubted that Terence was capable of looking after Cynthia properly, and his doubts were justified. He did his unsubtle best to prevent the middle-aged layabout – for so he considered Terence – from making off with his foul-mouthed but innocently trusting child. He put his foot down, but Terence's guile ensured that it was stamping on water.

'He told my father he was acting ridiculous. "She's of an age now. She can go if she wants to." Dad had to give in. He looked at Terry and he said to him, "Are you prepared to look after her and keep her, then?" Meaning of course, that he was washing his hands of us where money was concerned. "Are you prepared to support her?" Terry answered yes, though I think I remember there was a bit of a wobble in his voice. "Right, then, she's yours." And Terry's I was, or so I thought.'

Terence was still officially married when he appropriated Cynthia. He had no trouble persuading her to leave Hamilton and Melanie: 'I just needed to get away from home. I didn't feel really loved. I can't tell you how lonely I was. I was taken in by Terry. He came along at the right time and he knew it. He could see the state I was in and he made the most of it. But it was years before I realized what his game was.'

It is with hindsight, too, that she sees that she was marginally, very marginally, the more stable partner in the relationship. She had inherited certain of Hamilton's qualities, she discovered – chief among them a concern about being able to pay the rent when it was due. Terence showed no such concern. There were rows. She found herself trying to nag him out of his indolence.

Terence drifted from job to job and from pub to pub. Unlike Hamilton, who confined his heavy drinking to the weekends, Terry drank every day. 'Even when there was nothing in the kitty he always managed to find enough for whisky.' She noted the difference between the man who boasted about his achievements to his cronies in the saloon bar and the wretch who whined with self-pity in the dingy rooms they shared together.

'He didn't keep me at all. He didn't know how.' Cynthia went out to work. As his total lack of application to anything other than his own comfort became more manifest, so too did her worry about getting into debt. She heard herself lecturing her middle-aged lover. It seemed astonishing, but a girl who was not yet eighteen was reminding a man in his forties where his responsibilities lay.

'He told me I was impossible to live with. He said I was a Tartar, a bloody little Tartar. Well, somebody had to show some determination, and I suppose it was me.'

According to Terence, the affair broke up because Cynthia had to have her own way too much. 'It wasn't that. It wasn't that at all. I sensed that he only wanted sex. He only wanted to fuck me, frankly. It took a whole year with him for me to find that out, and even then I needed to believe it wasn't true. Even after we'd separated, I went on hoping that he really loved me. I told him not so long ago, when he had the bloody nerve to remind me how impossible I was, what a lucky bugger he'd been. There aren't many men over forty who can honestly say that they're knocking off a lovely young girl, and for nothing too. Most older men have to pay through the nose for teenage crumpet, I told him, but you got me for sweet Fanny Adams. "You never had to reach into your pocket," I said. "You was bloody lucky." I mean, I was seventeen, I was practically a virgin, and there was him with his marriage on the rocks and no future to speak of. "You ought to show me some bloody gratitude," I said.'

Following the separation, Cynthia still saw Terence intermittently. They had sex on each occasion. 'I was always sort of running after him. I thought I was to blame, you see. I didn't realize that I was too good for him. I do denigrate myself, and I thought I wasn't good enough – that Terry was right and I was wrong – so I was always running after him, trying to get him back because he was all I had. I realize now that I was the one who was precious, not him. I didn't think enough of myself. My father had downed me all my life. I honestly thought that I was nothing.'

3

'He looked like Christie'

Rather than return to her father, Cynthia decided to chance life on her own. She found a job as a waitress in Brighton, but soon relinquished it in peculiar circumstances.

'I was working at Lyons, the tea shop, when this man approached me. He was a little bloke, but he made out he was somebody quite important. He looked like Christie, the mass-murderer. "Why don't you come and live with me?" he said. "I've got a daughter who is very, very lazy and I need someone to keep the place clean." He told me he had a nice house where I could stay rent free. I believed him. He was terribly polite, quietly spoken – he seemed a kind old gentleman. I must have been bloody mad, because I gave up my job and left the furnished room I was living in, and I went off with him. I was desperate for kindness, I suppose. Well, his nice house turned out to be a basement flat. It was in a shocking state – there were hundreds of empty milk bottles everywhere, all over the floor. Christ, it was a slum, it really was.'

There was a girl in the flat, but she wasn't the old man's daughter.

'Jessie, her name was. She was eighteen, like me. The first thing Jessie says to me is, "He hasn't got no money. He just pretends all that." He'd tried to have sex with her, but she wouldn't let him. That first night I had to sleep in the same room as him. He started feeling me and I got very upset, I remember, and broke down in floods of tears. "O.K.," he said. "I'll leave you alone, only please don't go away." He didn't try to bother me in that way any more. Looking back on it, I think he was after turning Jessie and me into prostitutes. He brought a couple of men back to go with me for money, but I wasn't having any. I said no both times, even though I was bloody hungry. I couldn't get my job back because it was winter already. He wouldn't let me claim assistance money because he was claiming it himself and wasn't supposed to have lodgers.'

She remained in the basement flat for almost nine months.

'I stayed with them because I was lonely. He was a con man, old "Christie", a right bloody shyster. He used to rob gas and electric meters. He was supposed to be the caretaker for the rest of the house, looking after it while the owner and his family were abroad. His idea of looking after it was to take their pieces of china, even their bloody wedding photographs, and sell them to the local junk shops. The electricity had been cut off because he hadn't paid the bill, so when it was very cold, when it was brass monkeys' weather, he'd go upstairs and tear up the floorboards. Then the three of us would huddle round a blazing fire.'

Cynthia's acting talent was called upon occasionally. 'He liked to kid people that me and Jessie was his children. The few times he had enough of the ready to take us out on the town, I called him Daddy and snuggled up to him and played the doting little daughter. That was the only fun I had. Otherwise, life was one long bloody nightmare.'

There were days when she didn't eat. 'I used to lie in bed as late as possible. I thought, "It'll soon be afternoon, and then it will be evening, and perhaps we'll have some money for food tomorrow." Or perhaps not. A cup of tea was a luxury. We couldn't heat the kettle until we'd set a bit of floorboard alight. "Christie" would come home sometimes and give Jessie and me a couple of shillings each. I would spend my two bob on bread and jam, but Jessie would waste hers by going skating at the ice rink. It used to get on my bloody nerves, the way she squandered her pittance and then had the cheek to ask for a slice of bread and jam. I was too soft-hearted to deny her.'

Cynthia remembered that as a small girl she had scoured the beach for discarded lemonade bottles. 'People flocked to the coast after the war. They hadn't seen the sea for five years. They were far too happy to bother about returning their empties and picking up the refund.' Her father, on hearing of the manner in which she augmented her pocket money, gave her a severe reprimand. She was bringing the family into disgrace. 'I told him just before he died that he ought to have been proud of me. It was private enterprise, what I was doing.' In Brighton, in the winter of 1950-1, she went in search of bottles again. She didn't find many, though there were days when she amassed enough to cover the cost of a loaf, a packet of margarine and a pot of jam.

With his keen eye for the insulted and injured, 'Christie', the caretaker, increased the number of his charges to five. 'He brought home this down-and-out called Marcelle. Her name's stayed with me because of the waves. She wasn't French, she was a nut case. She had a deaf daughter who'd just had a baby. There was no room for them in the basement, so he let them sleep upstairs on what was left of the floor.' Marcelle wasn't French, but she carried some foreign bodies into the house: 'She was so dirty and grubby she made Jessie, who was a bloody slut, look clean by comparison. Jessie said to me, "He's been to bed with her and she's got fleas." I'll never forget, this woman had gone into our bedroom – Jessie's and mine, that is; "Christie" slept at the back – and when we went in after her, we saw all these nits and fleas crawling up the curtains. She'd used a towel (God knows what for) which Jessie and I dumped at the end of the garden – it was covered in bugs. Jessie had a row with him. "Get that filthy cow out of here," she said. "It's either her or me, so choose between us." "Christie" didn't want her to leave. It was Marcelle and her deaf daughter and baby who had to go.'

Their departure was welcome in that it meant that Cynthia no longer had to put up with their hungry expressions whenever she cut herself a slice of bread. 'They just stared at me.

It was bloody pitiful. I resented giving them food, because I was sure Marcelle's daughter was getting welfare money for the child.' While they were in the house, she hardened her heart against Jessie, who was told to stop skating or starve. 'I remember the old boy giving me sixpence once. I crept out of bed at nine o'clock at night and walked all the way from Ditchling Rise to the centre of Brighton, where there was this soup bar. You could buy a decent bowl of soup for sixpence. It was lovely and hot and it warmed me right through. I would eat it very slowly whenever I went there, to make it seem more than it really was.'

Hamilton was told nothing of her life in Brighton. He certainly made no attempt to discover how she was faring. She wrote him chirpy letters from Ditchling Rise, where she maintained standards of personal cleanliness ignored by her fellow inmates. 'I saved every penny I could lay my hands on to pay for my sheets to go to the laundry. I always slept in a clean bed. I had that, at least.'

Early in the summer of 1951, she found employment as a waitress on the West Pier – a job that she had been told would be hers two months before. 'I could have worked for Du-Barry's, the factory people, but the reason I didn't go into the factory was that you had to work a week for nothing in those days – they started paying you at the end of a fortnight. The second Friday. I didn't have enough money to feed myself so that I could do a proper day's work. I was bloody daft. I could have swallowed my pride and asked for a sub – I might have got it. But I didn't think. I lay in bed most of every day at Ditchling Rise until they was ready for me on the West Pier. You were given free meals as a waitress – that was something to look forward to. Meat and vegetables after months of bloody bread and jam – I can't tell you what a beautiful prospect it was.'

The 'beautiful prospect' at last became reality. 'Going into the kitchens and having wonderful food – oh, the elation I felt, the sheer bloody elation. One day I collected a few shillings in tips and that was wonderful, too, and though I had to wait till the end of the week for my £3 wages it didn't matter because I was eating. The woman who ran the restaurant, she was sympathetic – she felt sorry for me. She asked me what sort of conditions I was living in and I explained. I explained, but I just couldn't tell her the full truth.'

'Christie' was not happy that Cynthia was now relatively independent. 'He didn't like it. He was frightened that I was going to leave. He wouldn't take any rent off me. He wasn't a bad man. In his funny way, he looked on Jessie and me as his family, and he was scared, I suppose, that like other families we would soon split up.'

On one of her days off, the young woman of means travelled twenty-five miles to see Hamilton and Melanie. She wrote to her sister on her return:

My Dear Melanie

Well I arrived back alright the other night. What did the old man have to say all grumbles I suppose? It was nice to see you after all this time, but at the same time I was upset to think that you wanted to join those friends of yours so soon only after you spoken to me for a couple of seconds. You can always see those people at any time but not always me.

Perhaps you'll realize when you get older, that when Dad die's and its not all that far off, that there isn't anybody like your own flesh + blood. The only friend we ever had was our Mum, and now she isn't here with us we should be real *sisters* to each other and help one another when in trouble. I know, in the past I have'nt been what I should have been but that does'nt mean to say I dont regret it because I do. When your out in the world all alone you learn such a lot about people and life itself and it is'nt always nice either. Then you realize how well I know I do, how lucky I am to have a Father that cares for me, and a sister I think the world off, and do anything for, but so young in her little mind to understand. I cant exactly tell you on paper what I'm trying to say its very differcult.

I've been longing to see you both, but I expect with you I was soon forgotten. In my heart I know with Dad he wants to see me more then he dare show. Dad is a very funny person, I'm only just beginning to understand him,he's very much like me has an awful lot of false pride, but with working every Sunday its very differcult to get time off.

I'm earning roughly about £6 a week waitress of course, but that still is'nt what I intend to get this summer. Come over one Wednesday early if you can get round Dad, and its my day off too I'll pay half your fare as it will be a lot for you to pay out. Its 5/4 day return, and then I'll take you out to tea somewhere then perhaps to the Hippodrome thats up to you anyway, you want have to pay for anything. Write back soon telling me the scandle. Fancy Rose expecting a baby. I expect they are all thinking why I havent had one before now ha ha. Please send me Keiths letters to me which he sent you if you dont mind, I shall love to hear what he says ... Send them all in a package if you like also you *must* please send on my bathing costume, as Ernie that is one of Keith's pals is going to take me up to London to meet his people in fortnights time and I shall probably sun bathe. He's a very nice boy he holds the same position on board ship as Keith does Asst/Laundryman in fact he is the boy I mentioned who was wanting to write to YOU remember.

He's brought me a double string of pearls with diamonds in the middle. He's home next week ...

I hope to go to Yarmouth for a week and a week in London. So please dont forget to send the costume will you? I also go to Elocution Lessons now at 3/6 an hour do you think I'm improving or didn't you notice?

I'm putting an advert in the Argus tomorrow for a post which would mean going abroad, I hope if I get an answer the old man will give me his consent else I cant go unless. Then you would have plenty of nylons' thats if I had the money. How I'd love to go abroad thats always been my ambition when I've done that probably I shall be able to settle down, until I do I dont think I ever shall.

Well I think I've written enough excuse writing in pencil but I'm suppose to be working. Were not busy but the boss keeps walking up and down still I dont care he can only give me the sack. There's plenty of jobs now.

Cherrio write soon wont you?
> All my love
> Cynthia
> XXX

After the long, dark spell in 'Christie's' basement, Cynthia was beginning to regain her confidence. Nice boys like Ernie were paying attention to her, giving her presents. 'I was in a hell of a mess when I was living with the old man. I was looking for a genuine boy friend, but I never found one – I was a pretty little thing, though I say so myself – and I could never understand why. And there was "Christie" bringing these blokes back. There's one in particular I remember. He'd met the old boy in a pub and "Christie" had said to him, "I've got a girl at home. She's not on the game, but try her anyway." He offered me money, this bloke. I wouldn't do it, hungry as I was. He said to me, "I've got nowhere to sleep", so I said – you could still do that in those days – "You can get into my bed, but I'm not having any sex." I wanted his company, I was very lonely. "I'm not having any sex," I told him, "but we can talk instead." He said, "You could never do that", because men don't think you can be in bed and not have sex, because men probably can't. He thought that by the morning I would give in, that by then I'd be so excited I'd let him have it. He didn't understand, a lot of men don't, that for a woman it's different – a woman's got to be turned on emotionally. Well, I'll never forget, in the morning he said he'd never had a woman say that and carry it through. We didn't have sex, hard as he tried. Believe it or not, he was quite pleasant to me in the morning – you know, a man who hasn't got rid of his spunk can turn bloody nasty, but he didn't. He took me out for a walk along the pier and he even bought me a meal – really lovely, that was. He didn't give me any money. He said he would come back for me, but he never did. He probably would have got what he wanted if he had persevered, but I suppose as he didn't get it that day he thought I was a dead loss, so I never saw him no more.'

She left 'Christie' and Jessie to their unlikely life in Ditchling Rise and moved into a comfortable furnished room near the sea front. She worked hard and ate well. When the season came to an end, she was unemployed once more. 'I decided that I wasn't going to go through another winter like that. London was the place for me.' On September 6th, she wrote to Hamilton:

My Dear Dad hm hm.

Just a few lines to let you know I'll be home for a few days before I go to live in London for the winter season. It will be an opportunity for me to learn a bit more about nursing and at the same time learning a language which will unable me to being a stewedess. Thank you for letting Melanie come to Brighton last Wednesday I think she enjoyed herself she ought to have done seeing the money I spelt on her. It seems rather a pity to think I have to entice her with nice things before she'll come over. Still perhaps she'll change though I doubt it very much ...

Goodbye for now till next week.

Yours loving

Cinders

XXX

The move to London from Brighton took an entire week to effect. What money she had saved was spent on settling her rent in Brighton and paying her London landlord a deposit for a room in Hammersmith. 'I remember travelling up to London every day by train, carrying my few belongings. I managed to get on without paying my fare. I still don't know how I managed it, but I did. I took my bits and pieces up to London over four days, and I never had a ticket. To show you how bloody stupid I was, on the last bloody day I was stopped at the barrier by this fatherly man who said, "You've got no ticket." "No," I said. "That is an offence," he said. I got away with it through my cheek, my honesty really. I looked at him and I said, "I know. Don't do anything. This is my last day. I've been doing this all week." He looked at me in real astonishment, I mean he was bloody surprised. So he said, "Well, I'll have to take your name and address."

I gave him my new address in Hammersmith, but I heard no more about it. I wasn't prosecuted. I think the ticket collector must have taken pity on me. He knew I was telling the truth. You don't say bloody stupid things like that unless you're being honest.'

She had no difficulty finding a job. She was immediately taken on as a waitress in the restaurant at the department store Swan and Edgar. She paid £3 a week for the room in Beauclerc Road which she shared with a girl called Linda. 'I don't know why I did it, but I wrote to Terry and he came and stayed a couple of nights. He got into bed with me, with Linda sleeping only feet away. I felt ashamed. My father, when he heard about it, was absolutely disgusted. "You mean to say," he said, "you let him do that to you with that woman there all the time." Well, that's what happened. I had sex with Terry and I clicked. I'd clicked with him once before, and he gave me some pills – I don't know where he got them from – and I came on again after taking them. But this particular time he tried to arrange an abortion and I got scared. I couldn't go through with it.'

She was fortunate in her next employer, a kindly woman who owned a café in Whitfield Street. 'She let me work for her until I was eight months pregnant. She was really considerate. One day I was in such a state I got on a bus with no money on me and an inspector booked me and I had to go to court. She went to the court with me and told the magistrate about the troubles I was going through.' It was this lady who taught Cynthia the best way to poach eggs. 'I cooked hundreds of poached eggs every day. When I started running my brothel, I made sure there were always plenty of eggs in the kitchen. The girls get hungry and the customers often like a snack afterwards. I'm not much of a cook, but I do a beautiful poached egg.'

Terence contrived to steer clear of London and responsibility. The confident Cynthia who had left Brighton with vague ambitions to study nursing and to learn a language was in desperate straits once more. 'I met another con man, in a pub in Goldhawk Road. He would have looked like Richard Widmark if he hadn't been bald. He chatted me up and said he knew a butcher who let him have first-class meat on the cheap. So he started coming round to see me, and he'd bring a couple of lamb chops. I was thrilled to bits with that, being shown kindness, I thought he was showing kindness. He was getting his oats, mind you, even though I was eight months gone. Looking back on it, what's a couple of lamb chops for a fuck? He was another who got it easy. He was older, too, and I thought he was being good to me at the time. I had a hell of a job trying to get rid of him after he found out that my father had money.'

She wrote to Hamilton when the baby was due, after four months' silence:

What you have heard is true but I did intend to go through with it without you knowing. I'm afraid there's nothing you can do to help me as I've seen to everything myself. Thanks all the same.

I'm quite in good health I've been attending the local Clinic and hospital for 3 months. I also intend keeping the child and the Father of the child is Terry, who eventually I'll sue as I think he's trying to get out of it.

Well theres nothing much more to say only stop worrying theres nothing you can do about it. Love from Cinders.

His response to this letter was to visit her in London and tell her off for becoming pregnant. 'His attitude was, "You've made your bed, you lie on it." He didn't offer me any money, though he could see how poor I was. I hated having to ask him for anything, but I got so bloody desperate at eight-and-a-half months that I sent him a telegram. By this time I was only getting thirty shillings a week from National Assistance. "Please send some money urgently. Love, Cinders" that was the message. Back came five pounds, which went a long way in 1952.'

Help of a more lasting kind was provided by Cynthia's welfare officer, Sister Olive. 'She asked me if I wanted to keep the baby. I said I'd like to but I didn't think I could afford it. She said, "If you really want to keep it, I can help. Bring the baby to me and I'll put it in my home." "Home?"

I said. "What home?" "Mine. I run it. We'll help you get on your feet after the child's born." She put me in touch with Queen Charlotte's Maternity Hospital, and a lady almoner arranged for me to have the baby there.'

Three weeks before the child was expected, Cynthia went to Queen Charlotte's for a routine check-up. 'I'd been bloody mad again, I should have been going regularly. While I was there, they said to me, "You've got to come in tonight." I was scared. "Tonight? Why tonight?" Then this nurse told me that they'd found I'd got toxaemia; I could lose my baby. "We want you in now." Once I calmed down, I thought to myself, "At least I'll get a decent meal in here" – that's how desperate I was. The nurse was worried, I could tell. She kept saying, "You will come in now, won't you?" I said yes. I'd stopped thinking about the toxaemia. I was looking forward to my evening meal.'

Her evening meal, in her opinion, was no meal at all. 'It was a salad. I hated salads. I could just see this heap of lettuce, some tomato and beetroot – nothing to get your teeth into. "Got any food?" I said. "Eat it," they said – it was a bloody order. Then I heard someone say, "We're going to induce the waters to bring the baby forward", and after that I don't remember no more because they must have drugged me. I don't remember waking up properly till a week later. Whenever I woke up, I saw these spirit forms in my room – spirit doctors, spirit nurses. I was dead scared to tell anyone. When the doctors said, "Are you all right?" I answered yes, but I wasn't because I was seeing all these other spirit people behind them. One day I woke up and felt my stomach and suddenly realized I had had the baby. A nurse came in and I said to her, "What's the time?" She didn't reply. She just went over to the table and came back again. "What's the time?" I said, and still she didn't answer. Then a real nurse came in, flesh and blood, and it dawned on me that the other one I'd seen was a spirit. When I asked this nurse the time, she told me. "Do you think I could have something to eat?" – it's funny, but after all those drugs I'd been given, food was the first thought in my mind. "My dear," she said, "you couldn't keep anything down." I told her again that I wanted something to eat. When she brought me the meal – I can't recall what it was – I said to her, "I asked the other nurse to bring me something and to tell me the time, but she wouldn't answer me." She said "What other nurse? I'm the only nurse who has come into this room today." I felt really frightened then. "If I enlarge on this, they'll think I'm crazy" – that's the thought that came into my head. I was so terrified of what they might do to me medically that I thought, "I won't say it. I won't say it." I just clammed up. I saw those spirit nurses and doctors around me for days on end. I would put out my hands to see if I could touch them. When they came nearer, I ducked my head under the sheets, I was so bloody scared. As soon as I was awake, and the spirits were all gone, they drugged me again.'

Cynthia did not see her son until he was a week old. 'It was weird. They brought him in to me. I didn't remember the birth or nothing. And then I heard the nurse say, "Poor little thing. She's only a baby herself." Dominic weighed four pounds, that was all. What could you expect, when his mother hadn't been eating solid food?'

Tom, the provider of lamb chops, telephoned Hamilton with the news of Dominic's birth. 'My father rushed up to London, but I was too drugged to see him. He bought me hundreds of flowers – they were all over my room. He spent a bloody small fortune on flowers, but it was too late. I mean, I was putting bits of cardboard in my shoes because they were falling apart and he showers me with bloody roses. He gave me a couple of nightdresses – I was conscious when he brought those – and he handed me a little money, but the damage was done. He thanked Tom for keeping an eye on me, for letting him know how I'd been. Then he took himself home.'

Cynthia wrote to him soon after:

I'm writing to say hes going to be called Dominic Arthur now I've at last made up my mind. I did like Barry though but I think the other name is less unusual. The doctor said I was better today, said I could get up to have a bath which I asked if I could do. He looked at me and saw my make-up and the ROUGE lying on the locker and said, now are you sure your feeling alright your not just saying that are you. Then with a smile said, dont put any more of that stuff on else you'll set yourself on fire. Its terribly hot in this room I'm getting a little bit fed up. One or two of the nurse's makes me mad, I'm sure to answer one of them back one of these days. I know they do a grand job and work hard but these student nurse's they are always in a blinken hurry rushing about and when I feed the baby with the bottle the little devil plainly ignores me with those eyes, and flatly refuses to suck after he's had a little drop, and they say he must have it, then I have to force it down his little throat then he vomits it all up. It makes me all of a panic but I suppose I'll get use to all that. Then the nurse's are larky because I'm too slow feeding him, then it makes them all behind you see. I dont believe in forcing it down them but they seem too. I dont know when I'm coming out not before Wednesday, anyway. Ask Winifred for me if she'll let me stay with her for a few days at the end of September.

Well I'll close now give Melanie my love tell her I'll give her birthday present to her when I get out Cherrio thanks for what you've done love from Cinders

There follow eight kisses. Three days later, she sent him another letter:

Just a short note to say on Sat morning I shall be going to live with Sister Olive for about 2 or 3 weeks until I can find accomadation. I dont partucrrably want to go but I suppose if you have the sweet you got to have the bitter. Anyway they help you to learn how to look after the baby which is bound to be a help. It will be in Chisick not far from this hospital the lady Armourer has arranged everything for me. It will be better in a way because I will be allowed more freedom and visitors. You or Melanie could come up and spend three or four hours with me taking the baby out, as I'm allowed out every afternoon.

Well I'll write again if I dont see you before the weekend give you the address, find out how their system is and let you know.

Cherrio for now. Love Cinders

She was frightened at the thought of living in the Church Army home for mothers and babies, even though Sister Olive had assured her she would be cared for there. She definitely didn't want to go back to the room in Beauclerc Road which she had been sharing for nearly a year with the increasingly untidy Linda. She had written to Hamilton weeks before Dominic's birth begging him to break into the savings he had accumulated on her behalf – with them, she told him, she could rent an unfurnished apartment, where there would be no problem about having a growing child on the premises. Hamilton's reply to this pathetic request has not survived. He did not release the money. Perhaps he reasoned that his daughter might yet find herself in even worse circumstances.

Shortly before Cynthia entered Queen Charlotte's, Sister Olive had communicated with Hamilton, expressing her anxiety: 'I think she needs more supervision if she is not to go on making mistakes.' The welfare officer went on to say that the room in Beauclerc Road was not a fit place in which to raise a baby. She suggested that Hamilton should talk to her, Sister Olive, about Cynthia's future.

The two met and talked. If the sister offered him advice, as she most probably did, there is no evidence whatever to indicate that he followed it, for the girl who had gone to earth, so to speak, with a man who looked like Christie was to live even more grimly for the next five years.

4

'A carnival bloke'

Cynthia and Dominic were taken by ambulance to the Home in Chiswick.

'The driver dropped me at the wrong end of Barrowgate Road. It goes on for miles. I had to troop up the whole bloody length of it, holding my baby with one hand and a heavy suitcase with the other. I nearly took off when I found the place, I was so terrified. "Christ," I thought, "what have I let myself in for?" But after two or three days inside, I was laughing. I'll never forget, Sister Olive she came up to me and said, "Cynthia, I remember you saying you were scared to come into my home, and now you're screaming with laughter." She told me it was lovely to hear, my laugh: it was reassuring; it meant I was on the mend. I realized then that it wasn't so bad in there – at least I was getting my food. And good food it was, too – not more of those bloody salads.'

Of the dozen women in care, Cynthia was the only one who intended to keep her baby. 'It took guts to do that in the 1950s. The others were all worried what their parents would think and what the neighbours would say. Some of them had been pressurized by their mothers into having the kiddies adopted – to spare the family shame, that sort of blackmail.'

While she was in the home, she managed to shake off her third 'con merchant'. 'My father had slipped Tom a fiver when he thanked him for looking after me. Guilty conscience,

51

I suppose. Tom got it into his thick head that Dad was loaded and scrounged £15 out of him – more than I ever bloody got – to tart up an old van he'd bought.' She wrote to Hamilton:

> I've finished with Tom. I've just had about enough. One after another he wants stuff for that van and there he is doing nothing. About time he started to work to help with the payments. And that £15 you sent him. I wish you would always consulted me. I would have never had let you sent it to him. I *hate* borrowing money. I never knew anything about it. He knew darned well I would have kicked up a fuss. Thats no way to start any business. Melanie will tell you what happened. Tell her I said she can tell you. Admittly he probably spent it on the van but it was the lies I did'nt like. I shall go to work myself I'll manage somehow. Theres only one way to success and thats the hard way. I already said I've finished with him but one of the girls here have told me he's coming up the road to see me. I think he's sorry and I do believe he'll pay me some money when he gets some. I told him to sell the van, but I dont think I'll ever get that money what *I've* paid for it. But he's not going to fool me I can get on without him. It will be harder but its worth trying. Dominic is growing into a lovely boy I would never give him up even if I've got to scrub floors.

Tom was confronted by a determined and resolute Cynthia. He was not going to fool her, she announced. She could get on without him. She reminded him, as she had reminded Terence, that he had assumed certain responsibilities.

The acquaintance of the purveyor of first-class meat returned to his lodgings and dashed off a letter to Hamilton:

> I am so sorry about not writing before but I was so very Glad about you sending me the money and it all went on the Van. I have already showed Cinders the bills for it. I hope you dont think I am all for myself because I am not, Cinders has only got to say whether she wants to finish with the Van or not, I mean all said and done *its hers* and

as for trying to twist her out of it I am not made that way. We are getting on O.K. again for a change. I have got the Van O.K. its running lovly now, I am going to work for a while until I can get a few pounds so I can go down the markets with to do some business. I have put my heart and soul into that Van believe me Mr Payne. I hope you dont condemn me for not writing to say I received mony I apolize very much. I will send it back soon and thanks again. I hope Milanie enjoyed her stay in London Yours Sincerly TOM

Assisted by the always sympathetic Olive, Cynthia staged another confrontation at Barrowgate Road. 'She was a cute old stick. She told me to write to Terry and say that I wanted to see him. I wasn't to let on that I was being looked after in a mother and baby home. So I wrote to him on ordinary notepaper and just put 53 Barrowgate Road, London, W4 at the top. He fell for the bait, all right – oh, he fell for it hook, line and bloody sinker. He thought I was in furnished rooms. He didn't mind parting with the train fare to London so long as he could get a fuck at the other end, that's what I reckoned. He was knocking on the door of the home by return of post, if you see my meaning. Sister Olive let him in. She was a cute old dear. "Cynthia's inside," she said to him, without telling him where he was. "Go right in." She showed him into a waiting-room, didn't she? He must have been wetting himself. It was marvellous, it was really marvellous, getting one over on Terry after the way he'd treated me. I walked into that waiting-room and I said, "Hullo, Terry. This is a home." I sat and talked with him for half-an-hour and Sister Olive made some excuse to come in and she saw us talking – it was evidence, it was definite proof that he was the father of Dominic.'

Terence had lunch with Cynthia and Melanie on the day the affiliation order was brought against him. 'They always say just before you go into court you shouldn't mix with the defendant, and it only goes to show how true that is. He knew my sister was a witness, that she was there to say I'd been going with him a lot. He was the bloody mad one, for a change. We went to this little cheap café and Terry started up on his high horse and turned to Melanie and said, "I hope when Dominic grows up that he'll have the brains of his father, and not his mother." He could have bitten his tongue off. In court that afternoon the judge asked Melanie if Terry had ever said anything, ever, that suggested the child might be his. So Melanie said, "Well, about thirty minutes ago in the restaurant he did say he hoped the child would have the brains of his father rather than his mother." And that was how he got caught. That one stupid boast – or bloody sarcasm, more like – it did for him. He was ordered to pay me fifteen shillings a week towards Dominic's upkeep. I really needed that money, for the child's sake. But he seldom paid me, and he got it down to a shilling towards the end. Terry was a schemer. He knew I wouldn't go on pushing for the money because it was such a bloody effort to get it out of him.'

The schemer was aware that Dominic had an industrious grandfather. He felt safe in the assumption that Hamilton would ensure that the boy came to no harm. 'My father refused to pay whenever Terry let me down. "You've made your own bed, you lie on it." I used to take Dominic home two or three times a year, but Dad forbid me to bring him into the shop. He'd leave the garden gate unlocked for me. "I don't want people to know you've had a baby. I want to keep it quiet" – that's what he said. It was the tradesman's entrance for his own flesh and blood.'

Dominic's father had himself been abandoned as a baby. He had been left on the doorstep of a convent, wrapped in a shawl. 'He used to get tearful about the nuns. "I'm leaving all my money to that convent" – he said that the last time I saw him, about a year ago. "The money you forgot to give your son," I said. "The money you waste getting yourself bloody maudlin." He was crying for himself, as usual.'

Cynthia stayed at Barrowgate Road for six weeks. She was then sent on to another home, Torrington Park, where Dom-

7. Cynthia at home in Ambleside Avenue.

8. Roger relaxing in Cynthia's lounge.

VALUE
10p

VALUE
15p

9. Preparing for a party.

10. 'Luncheon vouchers'.

11. Making up before a party.

inic was cared for by the nurses during the day while his
mother was out at work. She stayed there a month.

She did not return to the prospective marketeer, who had
put his heart and soul into the Van. She lacked Tom's faith
in his own business acumen, particularly now that she had a
child to support. She began to fend for herself.

'It was bloody terrible. Any man who gave me a meal, I let
him screw me. I had to find lodgings where there was someone who could look after Dominic in the day time. One place
I went to, the husband started to take too much notice of me
and his wife had to get rid of me. People have got no idea
what it's like when you're stony broke and dependent on
people. When you're unmarried with a baby they think they
can take advantage. I shacked up with this bloke Charlie. I
lived in one dirty room with him. I left the baby with a
woman down the road and smuggled him in at night without
the landlord noticing. I stayed awake to all hours in case he
started crying.'

On April 16th, 1953, Sister Olive wrote to Hamilton:

> I am afraid Cynthia is not doing at all well, or looking after
> baby as she should – I haven't heard from her myself but
> I get bad reports from workers on the district where she is.
> It is all very disappointing.

'I had no money, that's why. There was no social security
to speak of in those days.'

Later that year, she gave birth to a stillborn child.

'It was Charlie's. We couldn't have afforded it, anyway. I
was having enough trouble keeping Dominic fed and clothed.
Charlie wasn't a con artist, but he was always skint. I went to
one welfare woman, I remember, and I said, "Look, I can't
look after the baby properly. I *am* trying, it's not that I'm not
trying." I suppose the kid *was* neglected, but he wasn't
cruelly treated – he was never bashed about or anything
horrible like that. It was just that he was having to live in
slum areas with slum families. I realized this was no good; I
realized this was no way to bring him up. He had to be
fostered out, there was no other choice. I put an advert in a

shop window in Holloway – I was living in a dirty rotten hole in Holloway Road. "Foster mother wanted for little boy." I never thought I'd end up in Holloway Prison, because when I used to pass it on the bus I would joke to myself, "You'll end up in there one of these days." You don't think jokes like that will come true, do you?'

Her advertisement elicited seven responses.

'One was from Hoxton, in the East End. It was worse than "Christie's" basement, the dump she lived in. It was shocking. It made our Holloway hole look like a bloody palace. I could never have left him there. This Mrs Somerville, she wrote to me, I knew at a glance her letter was genuine. She hadn't been able to have children. I went to see her. I liked her straight away. She took to me and she took to Dominic. I let her have him. It was the wisest thing I ever did. She charged me £2 a week to start with. She was very motherly.'

Life became relatively easier after Mrs Somerville began to take care of Dominic.

'It wasn't easy for long because I was pregnant again. Can you imagine – after all I'd gone through, here I was pregnant again. I mean, I wouldn't have minded if I'd enjoyed the sex. But I wasn't enjoying it. I was only doing it to keep a man. I thought he'd leave me otherwise. So there I was, getting myself in worse schtuck. I will say this for Charlie – he stuck by me. His only trouble was that he never had enough money; he was a casual labourer, and there were times when jobs were scarce.'

She gave birth to a healthy child.

'Charlie came from a broken home himself and he said to me, "We can't bring this boy up properly, so we'll have him adopted. You've got Dominic anyway." He found a couple who couldn't click and they took him. He was just weeks old.'

She parted from Charlie on reasonably amicable terms. 'Ours wasn't a flaming bloody passion by a long shot. We kept each other company, that was about the depth of it. We were both lonely. I lost interest in him, though. I wanted what I'd always wanted – excitement. I realized I'd miss out on that if I stayed with him. "I don't want any more. I'm finished," I said. He didn't make the slightest effort to persuade me. "Why not?" was all he said when I suggested we split.'

Cynthia arrived in Margate with ten shillings in her pocket. It was her intention to work as a waitress for the summer season.

'I'll never forget the first day I was there. I went into a hotel and I got a job as a chambermaid. I had to have a roof over my head – that was the main thing. At least I'd have somewhere to sleep. That night I dressed myself up, put some make-up on – the Yanks were in town, and I thought one of them might take a fancy to me, and give me a good time. Americans were never short of the spare. I went to Greenland Park, the amusement arcade. I was walking past a ball game when a voice said, "Come over here, darling." I said straight back, "You won't get any money out of me." That's how Sam and I got started. I was twenty-two by now. "Come here," he said. "No," I said, "I played that game when I was a youngster. You can never bloody win." "Come here," he said. "I don't want your money." He burst out laughing. I think he liked my savvy, because though I was green I wasn't going to let him have even a sixpence. He told me I could play a game for nothing and then he said, bold as brass: "Meet me later on at the main entrance. I finish at eight." I said yes, I would. We had a meal and he was good fun to be out with, and two or three days after he said, "Leave that hotel and come and live with me. I've got a nice flat." So I did.'

She was hired as waitress in a fish restaurant and lived with Sam until the season was over.

'Oh, it was bloody wonderful. He was a con merchant, too. He was a different kind of con man, though. He conned with class. He knew how to get people to spend their money. I used to sit and watch him. They'd spend pounds on his ball game. He'd fake it so they would win once in a while, and of course that made them go on playing. The oldest trick in the world, but they always fell for it. We had some lovely bloody laughs, the two of us.'

57

He said the first of several goodbyes to her at Victoria Station at the end of September.

'He had other woman, of course.' (Cynthia never refers to 'women'. The singular noun is made to do service for multitudes. 'Woman are more romantic than men' is a typical utterance.) Sam also had a mother, upon whom he doted: he lived with her in a tenement in the East End. 'He was very good to old Sophie. He used to say he would never let her go without. She was his excuse for not marrying me. "I can't afford you *and* her, and it's not in my nature to let her go without" – oh, he must have told me that a dozen times. I would have made him a good wife. I would have helped him save his money.'

During that winter in London, Cynthia discovered that she was pregnant. She contacted Sam, who insisted that she have an abortion. She complied with his demands. 'That first one was quite easy. There was no pain to speak of. It was all over and done with quickly.'

Sam was equally insistent on his right not to wear a contraceptive. His was an aesthetic objection: 'He said it was like going to bed with your socks on.' As a result, he impregnated her again the following summer, when they were living together in Margate. 'We bloody clicked, because he didn't draw out in time. "You can trust me, Doll," he said – he always called me "Doll", did Sam – "I'll be very careful." After that, I was too tense to enjoy having sex with him. "Why don't you bloody relax?" he'd ask me. As if I could, with the thought of ending up in the club at the back of my mind.'

Her second abortion was neither quick nor easy.

'The woman I'd gone to before wasn't available – I think she must have given it up. So we had to find somebody else. Sam got wind of another one who practised in Aldgate. You couldn't see her face for make-up, and her hair looked as if it had been dyed every colour of the rainbow. She was a really rough customer. I took against her the moment I clapped eyes on her, but I had to go through with it. I had no choice. And besides, she was cheap. She only charged a fiver. While she was getting things ready, I half expected Jack the Ripper to walk into the room – it was that bloody horrible. I was much more scared than I'd been the first time, because that first woman was clean. She was more than clean, she was pernickety – you know, fastidious. She sterilized everything, but not that Aldgate cow. All of a sudden, she – Aldgate, this is, with the warpaint on her moosh – well, she got a bowl ready and I could see she wasn't particular. Then she picked up a syringe and started to fill it with warm water and washing powder. I'll never forget that – she put Daz in the syringe. When you do an ordinary abortion with an enema syringe, you use a mild carbolic soap. I must have been bloody mad, because I didn't think nothing of it, except I remember her putting Daz in the water. I should have said something. She told me to stand over the bowl. What they do with an enema syringe is that they stick the tubes up because they know where to get to the womb – the first woman who did it didn't hurt me in the least. You could tell she was skilled; she knew what she was doing. When that second woman did it, though, I was really frightened. It hurt like hell. "That's all right," she said. "You'll come away. Come back and see me tomorrow if you don't." She didn't seem to realize the pain I was in, she was so matter-of-fact.'

Cynthia rented a room in north London in which to have the abortion.

'Sam kept well away from me. He was squeamish. "I'll leave you to get on with it" – that's how much he cared. I had no friends. I was all alone. I took myself off to the cinema that evening. Every time I had an abortion I would go and see a film, just to take my mind off what was happening. The pictures cheered me up. I saw *The Roman Spring of Mrs Stone*, I remember, and *Roman Holiday* – that was a funny coincidence, those two films being about Rome. I'll never forget, I was in agony that night after Aldgate. I had nobody in the house to confide in, the landlady was only interested in her rent, and I lay there in that scruffy room until the morning and the pain I was in was terrible. It was the Daz washing powder. The Daz washing powder had smarted my insides. I got out of bed as soon as it was light, I was still in agony, I managed to dress somehow or other, and then I wandered up

Finsbury Park Road to Lyons Tea Shop – very, very slow, because the pain I was in was terrible; I can't say often enough how terrible it was. I went into Lyons and I ordered a milk and a dash – they used to do a special coffee called a milk and a dash. It was the best thing I could have had, that warm liquid going through me. I didn't realize, I just wanted a milk and a dash, I craved nice hot milk and I didn't realize. I came out of Lyons and I started walking towards Seven Sisters Road and I caught sight of the toilets in the middle of the street. All of a sudden, I felt something dropping between my legs. I thought, "Oh, my God, the hot milk's done the trick." There I was, stuck in the Seven Sisters Road, with blood running down me, and I knew I had to make it to the ladies' pronto. I had this lump wedged between my legs, I don't know how I managed to walk. I kept stopping, because of the thing between my legs. I thought, "Oh, Christ, it's the baby." Abortions were illegal in those days, and if I'd come away in the street, in broad daylight, I could have been arrested. By some miracle, I got to the lavatory and found a free cubicle. It was very emotional – no sooner had I closed the door behind me than it came away. It was hanging between my legs with the cord. It was a boy and it was fully formed, so I must have been further gone than I'd reckoned. The first abortion I'd had, it wasn't formed, it was just a sort of lump, but with this one an awful feeling of guilt came over me because I could see it was a boy. I remember crying in the toilet and saying, "Oh God, forgive me", or something like that. I don't believe in God, but I remember asking Him to forgive me. I told Him I had to do it, I had to have it done. I remember wrapping the baby up in some newspaper and sticking it behind the S-bend of the toilet and I was weeping all the while. At the same time it was odd, I had a tremendous feeling of relief that the abortion was over, because I'd dreaded having another one. So I was really elated that it had come out, but I do remember crying and asking God to forgive me.'

She remained in the public lavatory until her tears had abated.

'I soon got over the God business. I had to start living

again. It was always a worry finding someone to do an abortion, and now the worrying was through I wanted to start afresh. I was still in pain from the washing powder, but I knew I had to get to Victoria and catch the train home. My father was expecting me. I had my suitcase with me and it weighed a ton although it was light because of the pain I was in. I could hardly walk. I remember I stopped a bloke and asked him if he would carry my case across the road. I told him I'd just had an operation, that's what I kidded him. He helped me on to the bus, and then I caught my train. Dad was waiting for me at the other end. I'll never forget, my father was impatient with me for walking so slow, slower than a bloody snail, he said. "Christ, Cinders, can't you walk quicker than that?" I was trying to keep it away from him what had happened. I thought, "If only you knew." I had no money, I was only home because I didn't have much money, and I knew I'd always get my food down Dad's as well as a comfortable bed with clean sheets. I really needed to lay in bed. My father was furious with me: "Get out of that bloody bed," he shouted up the stairs, "or I'll come and drag you out." He could never stomach laziness, and he wasn't to know that I wasn't being lazy. Oh, it was terrible, having to keep the truth from him. It was so painful just getting out of bed that in the end I confided in Melanie. I explained to her that I'd had an abortion, and I asked her if she could fetch me something – I can't recall what it was – from one of the other rooms. She got annoyed and said, "I'm not running about after you." I said, "Look, Melanie, I've just had a nasty abortion." I'll never forget, my sister was that hard, it still didn't make any difference to her, she wasn't sympathetic at all: "I'm not running about after you." Anyway, after two or three days, my father stopped nagging me. I think Melanie must have told him what I'd told her. If he knew, he never let on. He wasn't exactly affectionate, but he was treating me a little better. Not being bawled at made a nice change.'

Unlike Terence, who frequently welcomed Cynthia with open palms, Sam never asked his 'Doll' for money. Men were providers, however intermittently, and when they were short of funds they found a good excuse to disappear. Sam was constantly inventing such excuses.

Cynthia was in love with Sam, was obsessed by the 'right little grafter' to the extent that she allowed his every indulgence. 'I must have been bloody mad. He was a very sexy person. He'd want it morning, afternoon and night and it used to get on my bloody nerves – it was just too much. He gave me so much that I could never learn to enjoy it. "Why don't you ever have orgasms?" he asked me once. Well, I was scared of getting pregnant for one thing, and for another he didn't seem to understand that if he cared about *my* pleasure rather than *his* I'd stand a better chance of coming too. A lot of men just don't care about satisfying woman. Sam gave me so much sex I went off it for two or three years after we packed it in. It sounds daft when you think what I do for a living, but it wasn't until I was in my late thirties that I came for the first time – that was with Mohammed, who really knew how to fuck so that it was fun for both. Mind you, I was on the pill by then, which made life easier – I wasn't worrying all the time about clicking with Mohammed and having black babies by the cartload. But it wasn't like that with Sam. Even though I loved him, that side of life was never fun. I remember crying once while he was doing it because I didn't want it and I said so, it was that time of the month. He took no bloody notice. When the prick is hard, the brain is in the balls – and that's where his was. I used to get into bed with Sam and want him to cuddle me, show me affection, but of course a man like Sam couldn't cuddle for long without having a hard-on. I would say to him, "I'll let you cuddle me, but I don't want any of that, because I'm not in the mood." Then he'd say, "All right, Doll. I'm not going to do it. I don't fancy sex tonight either." The crafty sod. After cuddling me a little while he'd become so bloody hot, there was only one thing he could do to cool off. So in the end I'd give in to him and I'd never enjoy it. I'll never forget, he came home this particular afternoon and we had a bit of a row. He said he was ready for it and I said I wasn't. Anyway, I learned early on in our relationship that the best thing to do was to get him despunked. Sam was marvellous company as soon as he'd come – when his cock was soft he was a carnival bloke. With his brain in his balls, though, he was a bloody pest. I was really furious with him that afternoon, but I took my clothes off and lay on the bed and I picked up the evening paper. I thought to myself, "I'll show you how much I want it. I'll read the bloody paper while you're screwing me." And that's what I did. I tried to block my mind from the fact that he was fucking me. Oh, he went bloody mad. He flung that paper across the room and called me all the cows under the sun. But as I say, when he had his brain in the right place and plenty of money to spend on his Doll he was the most wonderful man any girl could wish for.'

Thanks to Sam's distaste for rubber wear, Cynthia had to undergo a third abortion. 'Sam would say he'd draw out, and sometimes he did, nine times out of ten he did – but when he didn't, I clicked. I'll never forget, Sam found another woman to do it. She must have been a friend of his, because she talked sense to him. "Don't you leave that girl on her own," she said. She was somebody with a mother instinct. She told Sam that if I died he would be in real trouble and that I shouldn't be left alone while I was coming away. I'll never forget, it was absolute bloody heaven: I remember Sam saying to me, "Look, Doll, I'm going to be with you on this abortion. I'm going to be with you all night." It was really lovely, having him there all night, because on the other occasions I'd always been on my own. He said, "You're not to do anything yourself. When it comes away I'll empty all the blood in the buckets. You're not to do anything. I'll empty the blood." I thought to myself, "Christ, somebody's been talking to him." So we had the abortion and we went to the pictures together and he took me home and I said it was going to come away that night and he said, "Don't worry, Doll, I'm staying with you." I wondered, "Why this sudden change?" but I didn't say anything to spoil it because it was really lovely. All night long I had the pains but they weren't bad, nothing like the Daz ones; the abortion had been done properly. I'll never forget, I got up in the morning and I said to Sam, "I think it's coming away", and then it did. It came down my legs. Sam hadn't seen it when it happened before. It was a boy again. We had this one big room and I was quite excited, I was elated. I said, "Oh look, Sam – it's a boy." Of course, thinking back on it, he was frightened. It's always frightening to a man and I was taking it so casual. Anyway, I said to Sam, "Come and have a look at it." He was still in bed. He'd had his arm round me all night and for once he hadn't bothered me for sex. "No, Doll, I don't want to look at it." I'd got a newspaper there and I spread it out and I laid the baby on it and as I did I was struck by its mouth. Sam had an Edward G. Robinson mouth, people always called him Edward G. Robinson because of his big mouth, and there was this baby – he was fully formed – with Sam's identical mouth. I said, "Sam, it's got your mouth. Come and have a look at it." He said, "No, I don't want to look at it."

'All of a sudden I seemed to grow up because I thought that Sam didn't want to look at it because he was frightened. I thought, "Yeah, I can go through this, I can suffer the bloody pains, I can come away by myself in a public lavatory, but you won't even take a look." I had the baby in the newspaper and I went over to Sam where he was in the bed and I put it right in front of his face and I wasn't aggressive, I said, "Look, Sam", and he said, "I don't want to see it. I don't want to see it." I'll never forget, he couldn't help seeing it, and it's a pity it hadn't happened before because tears welled up in his eyes and he was really taken aback and he was always a bloke who didn't show his feelings that way and he looked at it and he said, "Just to think," he said, "that was once my kid." And he looked at me, he was crying, and he said, "You know, Doll, I promise you I'll never ever get you like that again." What a pity, what a shame he hadn't said that after the previous abortions – we might have had a different relationship. He said it too late. I suppose my mind was slowly changing. I'd started to ask myself what it was all about. I thought, "I'm still not married to you. After four coming on five years we've only got one room in Muswell Hill." That was the turning point. I stayed with him a few more months and he made bloody sure we didn't click even though he still wasn't wearing a French letter but when the time came to go to Margate with him for the summer I put my foot down and told him I was staying in London.'

5

'An old boy in a Bentley'

On her twenty-first birthday, Melanie confidently told her father she would soon be marrying the man who had been courting her, without Hamilton's knowledge, for the last three years. Her fiancé, she revealed, was a police inspector named Kevin.

Hamilton did everything he could to dissuade his hitherto sensible daughter from making what he considered an impossible match. He knew Kevin well, and admired him, but the fact that Kevin was almost fifty surely militated against his being the right husband for a woman on the very threshold of life. So Hamilton reasoned, to absolutely no effect.

'There's nothing you can do about it,' Melanie said. She reminded him that she had attained her maturity, and was free to do as she chose. She had chosen Kevin.

Hamilton regarded Melanie's choosing Kevin as a deliberate act of rebellion. If it was, it was both perfectly timed and reasonably defended, as befitted the character of the rebel. There was nothing in it of Cynthia's impulsiveness. Melanie could counter his every protest with overriding logic. Kevin's qualities as a human being, she asserted, more than compensated for the relatively slight problem of the difference in age. He was offering her emotional, as well as financial, security.

Hamilton did not say as much, but he was clearly perturbed

66

that Melanie had followed her sister's example – albeit in a more responsible manner, since she at least was intent on legalizing her relationship. He took the girls' evident need for older men as a personal affront, an indication that they found him lacking. In Cynthia's words: 'We were looking for the father we didn't have.'

Melanie was never forgiven, in spite of the obvious success of her marriage. Hamilton continued to think of her as un-natural, even after he had come to terms – in more senses than one – with the fact that his other daughter was blissfully happy running a brothel. Melanie's single act of defiance rankled. He had grown accustomed to disobedience from Cynthia. He came to see that he had mistaken Melanie's compliance for respect, her solicitousness for affection. None of Cynthia's many and varied misdemeanours ever caused him such anguish. Four years earlier, on November 12th, 1951, shortly before she discovered that she had clicked with Terence, Cynthia had written Hamilton an admonitory letter:

So you think Melanie is getting house proud do you? Well I'll tell you different. Melanie is thinking of leaving you at the end of the month. You expect that girl to do to much for the money you give her. You would'nt find anyone living who would do her job for that money. I dont blame her either she's getting nothing out of it and your not exactly a pleasant person to work for. Just because you worked hard for your money you expect everyone to do the same. Your be in your glory if you thought I'd be swetting at work thats one thing I shal'nt do. Its about time you see a bit more reason and stop thinking and moping over yourself. Else your find yourself lonelier still if she goes away. There is plenty of people worse of than yourself and they can make a little happiness for themselves. You have such a lot to be thankful for really have'nt you? just think, you've got two lovely daughters I'm not kidding for the both of us either. You've still in good health and your not hard up. Hurry up and get married again in spite of

Melanie. She'll get used to it after a while. She'll play you up all the more if Melanie knew she was the reason.

Melanie's longed-for departure from Hamilton was expedited at a time when Cynthia was enduring her worst humiliations. In that same letter to her father, Cynthia made casual reference to the fact that Ernie had recently proposed marriage:

> ... the boy I told you about Keiths pal in case you forgot the one who dredges the dockside. He's 2nd Laundryman now. Well hes home I went up to his place for the weekend as soon as he docked and he does'nt know yet whether he's home for Christmas or not as he's trying to get on another boat. Last Sunday night he asked me to marry him so it does'nt look if I'm going to be left on the shelf after all does it, I did'nt give him an answer I dont think it would work out any way he lets me have my own way to much. You ought to see the presents he gave me, Chinese pyjamers sets and nylons it would'nt be worth it to me to upset him. I'm not in love with him for one thing anyway. Keith's not married yet so I've still got a chance. I cant imagine you Melanie ever getting married can you? little devil.

The 'little devil' did marry, of course – happily, lastingly; as did Keith, as did Ernie. Yet Cynthia cannot recall that she ever regretted declining Ernie's proposal, not even when Sam's thoughtlessness was causing her scarcely bearable physical and mental pain. Life with Ernie might well have been stable, but it would never have been exciting. There was nothing of the carnival in Ernie's personality.

The man who could have inspired her to dwindle into a wife entered into a disastrous marriage soon after his separation from Cynthia. 'He was a bloody fool and his own mother told him so. Old Sophie came to see me when I had my first house in Streatham – she didn't know she was drinking tea with a future madam; she might have choked otherwise – and she said, "Cynthia, I'll always remember you telling my Sammy to save his money and buy a house. That was the best advice anyone ever gave him." She said, "Sammy used to say that Cynthia was a nut case, but nut case or not the girl had her head screwed on where money was concerned." Sophie said she would have accepted me as a daughter-in-law, even though I wasn't Jewish. She saw that I had a place of my own with nice furniture and she said that Sam and his wife and their two kids had been living in a terrible dump in the East End. She was very upset because she knew that I would have been better for him. Sam was like Terry – he was a Jew, too – when he took me for granted. If I'd made him respect me more, he would have come round to marrying me in the long run. Old Sophie understood that as well as anybody. "If my Sammy had done as you told him," she said, "he would be worth a lot of money now." But he didn't, because he never thought there was going to be a tomorrow, like most of the men I've fallen for.'

Sam met Hamilton and Melanie once, on a brief visit to Cynthia, who was convalescing after the second and most grisly of her abortions. 'He didn't tell me his opinion of Melanie, though I seem to remember he couldn't believe we were sisters, on account of her being so posh. My father came home from the pub at ten o'clock, he wasn't drunk, he was tipsy – a bit squiffy-eyed – and I introduced Sam to him. I was always proud of introducing Sam to people, I liked them to know he was my bloke. Anyway, I'll never forget, my father said, "Hello." That was it: "Hello." Perhaps Dad had cottoned on that Sam had got me in the family way and was just being off-hand. There was a ghastly silence and then my father said, "Well, I'm going to bed. I'll leave you two down here." And upstairs he bloody went. I remember Sam saying, "I never understood, Doll, why you left home. Now that I've met your father I understand only too well." I told my father what Sam had said that night when I was opening my heart to him towards the end of his life.'

Cynthia was in regular employment at the Elm Tree Café in Victoria when Sam invited her to join him in Margate for the fifth summer in succession. 'He said, "You're coming with me, Doll, aren't you?" and the answer I gave him he didn't expect. "I've got a bloody good job, Sam, and I'd be a fool to leave it." Looking back, I think I would have been more tempted to go to Margate if it hadn't been for this old man I'd met, a very rich old man, Jocelyn his name was, who'd come into the Elm Tree, all unexpected, early one evening. He was in the demolition business, was Joss – that's what I called him instead of Jocelyn. He was my first real sugar daddy. He came into the café, which was a cheap place although the food was good, and he was togged up something wonderful. He was the kind of man who even wore a tie pin. "What's he doing in a place like this?" I asked myself as I went to wait on him. I mean, he was really distinguished, a proper toff. Apparently, the Elm Tree was the only restaurant that was open and he hadn't had a bite to eat for hours. I always had a smile for the customers so I gave him a warm smile and I said, "Yes, dear?" all nice and friendly. I could tell by the way he was looking at me that he liked what he was seeing. He wasn't ogling me or anything. It was clear to me that he didn't have a bunk-up in mind, and that made me feel disposed towards him because I was sick of sex. I wanted a good long rest from being screwed. "What would you recommend?" he asked, and his voice was pure bloody cut glass. I said the roast beef was very good; you couldn't have better for two shillings and eightpence. "I'll take your word for it," he said, and I brought him a big portion of roast beef. "Very nice," he said, and he left me a five bob tip, which was a lot of money in those days. I was lucky if I got a shilling from some of them. He thanked me ever so politely when he left.'

Jocelyn began to visit the Elm Tree Café every day for a late lunch.

'He would come in when things were getting quieter, when the rush was over. Signora Pulga, she was Italian, she owned the place and had her two sons working there, one cooking, one waiting, she said to me, "He's after you, Cynthia." I didn't need her telling me because it was plain that he liked the look of me. He didn't fancy me. He wasn't clocking me the way blokes clock you when they want to get your knickers off. Then all of a sudden he plucked up courage and asked me if he could take me out to dinner that night. I was still living with Sam at the time, so I hesitated before I said yes. He took me to the Café Royal. It was bloody lovely – wine with the food, coffee and liqueurs to follow. He drove me there, the old boy did, in his Bentley. I couldn't believe it. He treated me as if I was a lady. He told me that his wife had died six months ago and that he was very lonely as a result and that the only thing that gave him happiness was to entertain a pretty young woman. He drove me home, I'll never forget, and we made a date to have dinner again.'

Sam went off to Margate in the full expectation that Cynthia would change her mind and join him there.

'He was bloody mad with me. He was the type who had to have his own way in everything; he was a right mother's boy in that respect. He was thunderstruck when I said I was going to stick in London for the summer. "All right, Doll, it's up to you," he said, "but I bet you you'll be in Margate before the month's over." He was bloody wrong. After a month on his own, he came chasing up to London, pleading with me to go to Margate. If it had worked that way from the start, if he'd shown me earlier how much he missed me, I would have gone with him. I'd been too easy with him, it was in my nature to be too easy with men. He waited until I lost interest in him before he showed any interest in me. It was too late by then. Previous to that, I'd told old Joss about Sam and he said I should leave him. "I've shown you a different side of life, Cynthia. Which do you prefer – life in one room with that unreliable man or life with someone who pays you the attention you deserve?" I didn't know what to say, except that I thought Sam was my ideal man, I thought he was the cat's whiskers. But after a while I began to see the sense in the old boy's words: "Sam will always be Sam," he said. What's more, Joss wasn't bothering me for sex. All he wanted was a goodnight kiss. It was bloody wonderful, not being fucked as soon as you got home from work. So I told Sam straight that Margate wasn't on the cards. I was happy at the Elm Tree and I was staying put.'

Cynthia was not an anonymous waitress.

'I had some laughs at the Elm Tree. I used to have the

customers in fits at times, I was so bloody cheeky. I pressed my tits against the blokes' arms as I served them their meat and two veg. "Lovely grub," they said and they didn't just mean the food. Mrs Pulga would give me a good talking-to when she caught me at it, but I couldn't stop myself. What I enjoyed most was teasing her sons, Franco and Lauro. I was convinced that they were virgins, if you can call blokes virgins. Those Italian families can be very strict. When I went into the kitchen, I would shove my tits at Lauro and whisper, "How do you like those, eh?" I loved it when he blushed. Franco was the more outgoing of the two, but he couldn't lay a finger on me without his mother noticing. Her eyes were everywhere. The signora would get bloody furious with me sometimes. "You stop interfering with those boys," she said. Oh, we had a lot of bloody wonderful laughs.'

Cynthia grew accustomed to having dinner in an expensive restaurant after a long day waiting at table in the Elm Tree Café.

'My sugar daddy pampered me, he really did. He wasn't the kind of man who wines and dines you for a fuck at the end of it; he wasn't that kind at all. He was very honest with me. He told me he occasionally picked up a girl in the Bayswater Road – they was working the streets in those days – and paid her £10 for a quickie. But he said he would rather spend the money giving his Cynthia a good time; it gave him much more pleasure. I was with him two years, my old boy in a Bentley. I started to feel guilty, I remember, about not going to bed with him, so one night I did. It was a bloody disaster. He was almost frightened to touch me. He only had a little cock – not that that matters; my lovely squadron leader didn't have a big prick either. Mitch offered quality rather than quantity. Anyway, I'll never forget, Joss had no idea what to do with it. He tried fingering my pussy, very gentle like, thinking it would excite me, but he'd been out of practice for so long that he didn't know what he was doing. He really didn't have a fucking clue.'

They paid frequent visits to a smart night spot in Maidenhead.

'Skindles was Skindles in those days. I mean, it was the élite place to go. I had the life of a fourteen-year-old when I was out with Joss. He taught me how to behave in polite company, and which bits of cutlery to use with which course – in the Elm Tree, you were just given a knife, a fork and a spoon, no fancy silver at all. I became like a Swengali, I really did, I even began to talk better and my family noticed it. He talked nicely and I learnt off him and I loved being in his company. What happened was, he really wanted to get married again, and I didn't particularly want to marry him. He was very much a snob – he wanted me to go to elocution lessons. He wanted to be proud of me. He used to dress me up and he was proud of me that way. I was still a pretty little thing, for all I'd gone through. So long as I didn't open my mouth, I didn't look out of place in Joss's Bentley. I never let my finger nails grow in those days, which was a mistake on my part, I realize now. Joss used to say he loved finger nails on woman; that was his fetish, looking back on it.'

Sam reappeared, after a long absence. He suggested to Cynthia that they should go on holiday together, to some romantic spot abroad, and try to patch things up between them.

'We went off to the South of France. We'd never been out of England in our lives, Sam and I, so off we went. "We always promised ourselves this holiday, Doll" – those were his words. He didn't take me, mind you – I paid my share and he paid his. I thought to myself, "I'm going to have a bloody wonderful time for once in my life." I'd kidded Joss, my sugar daddy, that I'd gone off on holiday on my own, but unbeknown to me he'd found out which hotel I was staying in and that I was there with a bloke. He didn't realize it was Sam. If I'd been honest with him and told him it was Sam, he probably would have understood. I kept it back, though. I must have been bloody mad, not telling him the truth. I know now that the older a man is, the more jealous he can be – he feels insecure because of his age. Anyway, I'll never forget, that first night in the South of France with Sam. There we were in bed in the hotel, and of course he wanted the other. I probably gave it to him: "Get it over with," I thought. "He'll be all right as soon as he's despunked." I was wrong. I'd forgotten what a sexy sod he was. He'd hardly smoked a cigarette before he was hot for it again. I told him straight that I didn't want it, and I'll never forget, he had to pass a remark on it, he said, "I don't know, Doll, we're in the South of France, we're in all this luxury, I'm in a hotel room with you and you don't want sex with me." He said, "All right, then, girl, there's a lot of French tarts in Nice." He got up and he put his suit on. "There's no argument," he said. "I'll go out and get a girl." That suited me fine. He came back after an hour, took his clothes off and went to sleep. I'd given him enough sex, what *I* thought was enough, but it wasn't enough for him, I suppose. I was dead sexually when I went away with him. I was uninterested. So our holiday passed with Sam spending most of his money on prostitutes in Nice. The rest he spent in the casino. Somehow, I wasn't happy with him. Something had gone. We drifted apart as soon as we were home again.

'Because of that bloody holiday, I lost my sugar daddy. Joss didn't believe I'd gone on my own, and when I finally let it out that it was Sam I'd been with, he still thought I was having him on. He was very possessive, as only an older man can be. I call him my sugar daddy, but he never gave me a lot of money – he used to pay the rent on the place I was living in near Victoria, he was generous that way. I really loved that old boy. I rang him up the day I got back to England and I said, "Aren't you going to come and see me?" and he said, "No, I'm married now, Cynthia." I couldn't bloody believe it. I'd been abroad less than a fortnight and here he was with a wife. I said, "What?" He said, "I've married a French woman." I yelled down that phone, "She's only after your money, Joss. She's only after your money!" He said, "Don't you dare talk about my wife like that on the telephone." I said, "Your wife! I've been with you two years, and you haven't known her five minutes." God, did I yell at him. "Don't you realize," I said, "that it's because I love you that I'm not your wife?" I knew I could never be posh enough to make him a proper wife. I'm not cut out to be a duchess type of person. I said, "I'm the one that loves you – not her. You can't have known her very long – she's only marrying you for your money. It's because I love you that I'm not your wife. Can't you see that?" He went very quiet on the other end. Then we just said goodbye. When that happened, I was so shocked because I felt he'd deceived me, though I suppose I'd deceived him myself by going off on holiday with Sam. I tried all ways to see that old boy again. I couldn't. He was a very faithful sort, and now that he was spliced he wouldn't agree to meet me. He wanted a woman to help him with his business, and I suppose he knew that I would have been a dead loss at playing the posh hostess. Besides, he liked to go to bed at ten o'clock most nights, and I was still a youngster. After Joss deserted me, I seriously thought about going on the game. I just had to find the nerve to get started. I thought, "Fuck it, I'm not bothering no more about love. It's for the money now." I'd lost my chance with Joss, and I couldn't expect another old boy in a Bentley to turn up out of the blue and invite me to dinner at the Café Royal. Miracles don't happen that often. Not in my experience, anyway.'

6

'I was terribly withdrawn'

The old boy in a Bentley was not the only acquaintance Cynthia made while working in the Elm Tree Café. Two of the restaurant's regular customers – Jeffrey, whom she calls 'Little Jeff', and Roger, who now acts as her unpaid chauffeur – became her close and constant friends.

'They're like brothers to me. Oh, I had an affair with Roger, but it wasn't what you'd call flaming bloody passion. I enjoyed having him in my bed. I couldn't get involved with him, though – not after Terry and Sam. Actually, I thought Roger was a right bloody drip when I first met him. I had trouble hearing what he was saying when he could be bothered to open his mouth. He used to talk into his shirt – it got on my nerves, the way he spoke. I'll never forget, one night when I wasn't in the mood for sex, I had a heart-to-heart with him. He talked all right then. I realized he wasn't the drip I'd taken him for – it was just that he was shy and afraid of making a fool of himself.

'Little Jeff's the quiet type, too. He's a tower of strength, small as he is. I put him in charge of the catering when I used to give my sex parties. He was a proper artist with the cheese and ham rolls, and the speed on him when he spread the butter took your breath away. He was a wonderful barman, too – he always wore a smart jacket and a bow tie, and he could tell at a glance when one of my gentlemen started to get squiffy. Nobody ever got nastily drunk at my sex parties, and it was mostly thanks to clever Little Jeff.'

Both Jeffrey and Roger look up to Cynthia and are happy to take orders from her. 'What with Terry first, and then Sam, and Joss chucking me over for that French woman, I was convinced that there wasn't a single man in the whole wide bloody world that I could rely on to look after me. I became my own boss, though it took a bit of time. Roger and Little Jeff do as I tell them and they don't seem to mind. That's just as well, because if they did they'd soon be told where to get off.'

One evening in the Elm Tree Café, a woman whom Cynthia had served on many previous occasions started a conversation with her.

'I didn't know she was a prostitute. She certainly didn't look as if she was on the game. She was about forty and she wore hardly any make-up. She seemed quite respectable. "Do you live in Victoria, dear?" she asked me, ever so casual. "Yes," I said. "Just a stone's throw from here, really." Then she wanted to know if I worked evenings, and I said I did. I was still in the dark about what she was on about, what she was after, "Well, my dear, I'd like to use your room for my business," she said. "I'll leave before you get back from work and I'll pay you £3 an evening." I thought, "Blimey, this is easy money!" I was being paid £3 a week in the Elm Tree and here she was offering me £3 a night. "I'll keep your room clean, dear. You won't know I've been there. You've got a wash basin, haven't you?" I told her I had. "Can I start tomorrow then, dear?" I said she could, and she slipped me the first evening's money in advance.'

As a result of this encounter, Cynthia decided to become a landlady of sorts.

'There I was, making this extra cash from the prostitute and putting the money straight in the bank. So, one day, I had what I thought was a brainwave. Why didn't I hire a small flat and let it out to a prostitute who preferred not to work at home? I got the place easily – there were always flats and rooms on offer in Victoria in those days. I had a banker's reference to help me, and very few girls who were on the game had one of those. I'll never forget, I went up to Park Lane and I chose the prettiest girl I could find and I asked her if she needed somewhere to take her clients. We got talking and we made a deal. I paid £10 a week to the proper landlord, and I charged her £20. I reckoned I could make a nice little profit that way, and not have to worry myself sick earning the necessary for Dominic's upkeep and education.'

Within a matter of months, she was letting out four flats – all of them in the vicinity of Victoria Station.

'I should have become bloody rich, but I didn't. I had to pay the landlords regularly, if only to keep their noses out of the flats. I kept my side of the bargain, but not the girls. The only one who ever paid on the nail was the one who used my room. The others were terrible. Whenever Roger went round to collect the rent, they always had some bloody excuse why they couldn't cough up. They gave him some real bullshit. The truth was, no sooner had they got the punters' money than they was wasting it on drink and drugs. If I'd known the trouble I was going to have, I wouldn't have gone into business. I had the idea I was on to a good thing, it was cast iron proof, but I was wrong. I hate it when people don't play fair, and those girls were making more than enough over the odds to afford to pay me on time. Thanks to them, I found myself in debt in the end, because I was having to pay the landlords a month's rent in advance and they were sometimes more than a month late in their payments to me.'

Cynthia befriended a notably reliable prostitute called Martha.

'When she had a place of her own, I became her maid. I answered the phone and opened the door to the men. I watched her closely because this was a new world to me and I was just a beginner. She was very curt with her customers; she never pretended to be affectionate. "You can't kiss me," she would say to them. "You can do what you want, but I won't be kissed." When I started running my brothel, I made it clear to my girls that I preferred it if they kissed my gentlemen. I like a girl to be loving on the bed, and there's nothing more loving than kissing to my way of thinking. But Martha was hard with the men, and it showed. Mind you, some of them wanted to be humiliated so much they were excited when she spoke to them in her headmistress's voice. She had a lot of what are known in the trade as Golden Rain clients – blokes who want to be peed on. Some days she had to drink gallons of tea to keep up with the demand. "Here's another one, Cyn. Be a love and put the kettle on." Oh, I was shocked, I can tell you. I only knew about straight sex in those days. I thought that all a man wanted was to fuck a woman, because Terry and Sam didn't seem to have much else on their minds. I was very much mistaken. I've learned different since then. Nothing shocks me now, though I have had one or two requests that have stopped me in my tracks. It's all human, in my view. You may wish it wasn't, but then again we don't live in paradise. A couple of Martha's Golden Rainers, and a few of her normal blokes, took a shine to me, but I said no to them. I'd have died at the thought of peeing on someone, and I was earning enough as a maid without having to lie down on a bed to make more. My business dealings hadn't turned sour and I was still seeing my old boy in a Bentley. I wasn't to know that life was soon going to knock me sideways.'

Cynthia's career as a leaseholder ended as abruptly as it had begun.

'I was too soft with the girls, and Roger was too pleasant to be a good rent collector. He couldn't scare a bloody cat. All of a sudden, the money wasn't coming in and I panicked. I gave the girls the heave-ho and got myself shot of all the flats but one. I'd given up being a maid by now. I didn't know what the hell I was going to do. The bills were piling up and, as I say, I panicked. I had this six-room flat I was living in with Roger and I remember I had this sudden fear that I wouldn't be able to pay the rent. I'd always paid my way, and now here I was, skint. I couldn't ask Joss any more, and Martha had her own rent to find when I tried to tap her for a loan. I felt really bitter. I was frightened, too, about the landlord coming round and demanding his money. I don't know why I worried so much, because he couldn't have got me out, but worry I bloody did. I'll never forget, Mr Fox, that was his name, rang my bell and I went and opened the door and he said, "I've called about the rent." I invited him in and I told him straight out that I didn't have it. "Let's discuss this in the lounge," he said. I caught his meaning. Martha had a flat in a block up the street and when she was short of the ready when the rent was due she would give Fox a free fuck. Without saying that that's what he wanted, he more or less implied that we could discuss things better if I drew the curtains. We sat on the sofa and he got very close to me. I was a bloody fool, because he was a decent bloke and if I'd said to him on the doorstep, "I'll pay you next week, or even next month", he would have been all right, I'm sure. But I didn't. I let him in, and of course he expected that I would behave like Martha, who he knew was a pro. I'd been her maid, but I'd never gone with a man for money. Anyway, he snuggled up to me, and I felt awful. I can't remember whether I wanked him or if he went the whole way, but I know he took advantage and I felt awful. It's what I was feeling that I can't forget. It was the first time I'd done anything like that. I gave in to him because I was frightened that he was going to tell me that I had to go. After he left, I felt absolutely awful. The thought that went through my mind was, "Well, I've done it." I'd refrained from doing it all these years, and now at last I'd done it. I thought, "Christ, even though I've got no money, I've done it." It was the breaking point. I realized I could do it and make money at the same time. I was so upset about it, that one incident. I'd made the decision to go on the game after Joss had thrown me over, but that one incident with Mr Fox was the breaking point. It made me bloody determined. I was never going to go crawling to people for money again. I had that other flat in Paddington and it was me, Cynthia Payne, who would be doing business there.'

Cynthia chose as her maid a permanently distressed lesbian.

'Dolores is a kind soul, but she's no bundle of fun and that's the truth. She can be in a room with fifty people all laughing their heads off, and she'll be the only one who doesn't see the joke. I've seldom seen her smile even. She's the perfect funeral guest, Dolores is. She'd look more miserable than the mourners. She used to get on my bloody nerves sometimes. "Here, crack that face, Depression" – that's what I'd say to her when she was deeper in the dumps than usual. She's very mannish, Dolly is – I've never known her wear a dress or a skirt. Always has her hair cut short. The funny thing is, a lot of my clients fancied her. There she was, looking butch and gloomy, and some of them had the nerve to ask her to whip them or beat them up. And these were the same blokes who had come to me for a plain, old-fashioned fuck. She has a lovely speaking voice on the phone, so the customers thought they were coming to a really classy establishment. Anyway, I'll never forget, I told her that I was going on the game. She knew all about my business activities, but she was genuinely shocked that I was thinking of becoming a prostitute myself. "You're *not*," she said. "You *can't*." "I can," I said, "because I've bloody well got to." That first day in the flat, my nerves were really on edge. I kept sending Dolly out for quarter bottles of gin. I'm not much of a drinker, but I needed Dutch courage that first day. I can't remember how much I knocked back, but I couldn't get pissed, hard as I tried. "Go and get another one, Dolly." And down the stairs she went. She was up and down like a yo-yo all afternoon. And the more I drank, the more of a state I was getting into. I'd had two babies, three abortions, I'd been a prostitute's maid, and still I couldn't make the switch. "There's a man arrived," Dolly said, so I said, "Show him in." I lay back and I let it happen, but I kept him talking for an hour afterwards because I didn't have the wherewithal to ask him for money. It was him who mentioned it in the end. "You do charge for your services, don't you?" he said. He was well-spoken and he had nice manners and I can remember thinking that if all the blokes were like him then life as a pro wouldn't be too bad.'

Roger was unaware of the precise nature of her employment.

'He thought I was out waitressing. I used to leave for work in the mornings wearing a black dress and a white apron, and I'd come home at nights in the same outfit. I didn't want him to know what I was doing, so I kidded him I was working at the Connaught Rooms in Victoria. If he was in when I got back at night I'd spin him a yarn and a half about having been on my feet all day, when the truth was I'd been on my back. Little Jeff was the first to hear what I was up to. I burst into tears when I told him. He was surprised, because he'd only ever seen me in a happy-go-lucky mood or in a foul bloody temper. Tears were the last things he expected. He talks about it to this day, because I don't think he's seen me cry since. God knows I've had enough to cry over, but I haven't – at least, not in front of other people. "I'm only doing it for three months," I said to Little Jeff. "Just to get the bills paid." I had to tell Roger eventually, and he didn't like what he heard, but he knew he had to lump it, he had no choice. I didn't tell anyone else. I was ashamed, that was the reason. I meant what I said to Little Jeff about not doing it for long. I just wanted to make a quick pile and then settle down to something respectable. But Dominic was growing up and I had to find the money to send him to boarding school and apart from being a waitress, which didn't pay well unless you were in a posh West End restaurant where you got large tips, I couldn't think of anything else I could work at that would bring in so much. It's bloody hard work, I can tell you, being nice and friendly to one bloke after another. I'll never forget, I made a terrible mistake to start with. I was short of clients, so I placed an advertisement in a tobacconist's window in Edgware Road. "French Polishing" was all it said, plus my 'phone number, of course. I should have put "Large Chest For Sale" or "Erection and Demolition", and then I wouldn't have had any trouble. I didn't know what "French Polishing" meant – I honestly thought it was a fancy phrase for a fuck. Imagine my surprise when a gentleman insisted that I give him a gam. "I don't do that," I said. "Then why advertise that you do?" Suddenly it dawned on me that I was selling myself as a plater. I've never enjoyed going down, and I only put my heart into it when I'm in love with someone. Anyway, I told the bloke that I would be happy to suck him off so long as he wore a French letter. He didn't look too pleased about that, but he could see that I was serious. He didn't pay me a second visit. It was the same with all the other fellows who turned up expecting a French polishing: I made every one of them wear a rubber raincoat. No wonder none of them came back! They must have thought me a right bloody cow, a real con artist.'

Cynthia's career as a French polisher was, of necessity, brief. It was Roger who, quite accidentally, solved her problem about the shortage of clientèle.

'He was working at Victoria Coach Station at the time. He came home one night and he said, "Here, Cinders, take a look at this." It was a little magazine called *Penny Black* – at least, that's what I think it was called. I'd never seen a contact magazine before. Roger had found it under a seat in one of the coaches, and was all set to throw it away when he flicked it open, casual like. Every single page was full of these tiny advertisements, no more than a line or two: "Severe mistress provides corrective training", "Virgin male requires mature woman for sex education", "AC/DC couple seek similar for foursomes" – that sort of thing. I read it from cover to cover, and I can't say I understood all the ads, because compared to some of those people I was really rather innocent. They used expressions I'd never heard of. I asked Roger if I should take a chance and he said it couldn't do any harm – it was a bit more bloody discreet, he said, than sticking a card in a tobacconist's window. So I sat down and I thought very carefully about it. I really racked my brain, trying to find the right words. I knew two I wasn't going to use: I'd done enough French polishing. I think I wrote that I was buxom and petite, which was no more than the truth, and that I'd like to make the acquaintance of interested gentlemen. I sent off my advertisement to the magazine with a postal order and they replied that they would put it in with a box number and would be forwarding all correspondence in due course. Oh, I was on edge for days; I can't describe how on edge I was, waiting for those letters to come. I didn't believe I'd get any, to be honest. And when they came, I was bloody bombarded with them. I was flabbergasted. I was up night after night writing replies. I had to let the blokes know, tactfully like, that I wasn't doing it just for pleasure: I charged for my services. The mention of money put a few of them off, I have to admit – but there were plenty who were happy to pay. A lot of the blokes I met at that time have stayed friends with me, mainly because of my sex parties, though some were surprised when they found out that I enjoyed being a madam. Men are funny about prostitutes. If a man's got a girl all to himself in a room, he can feel protective to her if he wants to. Many blokes were like that to me: they thought I was a helpless little thing. But when they saw me, years afterwards, at my parties, giving orders to my own girls, they weren't pleased by the difference in me. They only fancied me when I looked bloody helpless, I suppose – I appealed to their masculine pride. They didn't like to see their petite and buxom Cindy behaving like a shrewd businesswoman. That was only some of them, though. The rest agree that I found myself when I started organizing sex for other people.'

Being a prostitute, Cynthia discovered, meant having to change one's address with depressing regularity.

'I traipsed from flat to flat. I had dealings with a couple of landlords who were right bastards. They knew very well what work I was doing, yet they took my rent in advance and a bloody deposit, too. They let me get on with my business for about a month or so, and then they asked me to leave. They were shocked to learn, they said, that I was using their premises for an immoral purpose. They weren't bloody shocked at all, because both of their places had been tarts' parlours long before I used them. They wanted to get me out quick, so that they could get another girl in. I was threatened with the police, both times. I had no alternative but to leave. Anyway, I got wise to that particular racket. After that treatment, I decided to take Dominic along with me whenever I was looking for a new flat. I dragged Dolores in as well. She was the last person in the world you would think had anything to do with prostitution – with that mournful bloody face of hers, she helped me no end to come over as respectable. I passed her off as my companion: we'd been very close at school, I said, and when she heard that I'd gone through a divorce, she'd rushed up to London to take care of me and my little boy. She was bloody wonderful, Dolores was, at spilling a sob story: you felt that any minute she was going to shed buckets. She didn't have to act; she was a natural. Oh, I laughed myself sick as soon as I'd signed the lease. Even Dolores managed to move her lips a bit. "Go on, Depression, let's have a smile," I would say to her. "I *am* smiling, Cinders. Can't you see?" "I've lost my magnifying glass, Dolly, I'm not sure I can." Thinking back on it, I was bloody rude to her when the mood was on me.'

Despite the fact that the majority of her clients were congenial – even, as she insists, protective – Cynthia was deeply discontented during the two years or so she worked as a prostitute. She found herself unable to play the 'game' with much enthusiasm.

'I used to lay there like a log. Oh, I would smile, and I'd do my best to encourage a bloke who didn't have staying power, but really my mind was miles away. I was terribly withdrawn. I felt cold inside. It was like doing exercises all day long, except that I wasn't what you would call energetic. I was suppressing my personality. It was as if I wasn't being allowed to show the world the person I knew I was, the Cynthia who'd given herself to Terry and Sam. While I was on the bed I was nobody, hard as I tried to look loving. The men never guessed the state I was in, because I was too bloody good an actress to let on that I was miserable. I was professional in that respect. I had my future to consider, as well as Dominic's upkeep. I was determined to stay in control of myself, and make enough money to live the life I wanted. I was going to survive, somehow or other.'

Cynthia was always regular in her payments to Mrs Somerville, who had proved herself to be the ideal foster mother. Dominic was not only clothed and fed, he was also the recipient of genuine affection: 'He was shown more love as a child than I ever was.'

The boy prospered moderately well at the boarding school in Sussex to which he had been sent by a proud Cynthia. 'I wanted nothing but the best for him.' A report survives for the autumn term, 1961, when Dominic was a little over nine years old. The subject at which he excelled was mathematics:

'He learns rules quickly now and his work is always neat and well presented. He did a good examination.' Dominic's interest in maths still flourishes, in fact: he is at present employed by a finance company in the City.

His progress in English, history, geography and scripture also gave cause for favourable comment. His games master observed, 'He approaches football with keenness, and shews ability.' The one note of criticism is sounded by the form mistress, who considered him 'Co-operative and helpful as a general rule', and added, 'but can be obstinate.' This capacity for obstinacy appears to be the sole trait that Dominic has inherited from his mother.

Dominic continued his education at a secondary modern school in London, where he applied himself and earned good results. His greatest friend was a black African boy, whose charm Cynthia found irresistible. So close was their friendship that Cynthia began to worry when her son wasn't going out with girls – he was happy enough spending his evenings in Ezekiel's company. 'He was a really lovely lad, Ezekiel. He had girl friends, all right, but Dominic didn't seem to be bothered with them. I started to wonder if he was in love with Ezekiel – in a physical way, I mean.' To put her mind at rest, she gave him an unusual present on his sixteenth birthday. 'I handed him a ten pound note and a piece of paper with an address and 'phone number written on it. "You ring that number, Dominic," I told him, "because that's where you're spending the tenner." The poor sod looked ever so confused. "She's expecting you, so if you don't turn up I'll hear all about it." "Who's she?" he asked. "You'll soon find out. I can guarantee you'll have a nice surprise." I'll never forget, I'd arranged with a beautiful coloured girl who was on the game that she should take my Dominic's cherry. I was convinced that he was still a virgin, and I wanted him to be broken in by someone who was really experienced. Oh, I was bloody excited when he set off that afternoon, you'd have thought I was about to have the fun, not him. I couldn't wait for him to get home again and tell me what had happened. As it was, the girl rang me and said that he'd passed the test; he was normal beyond the shadow of a doubt. "Did you enjoy

Evening

STANDARD

CLOSING PRICES

on : Monday
21, 1980
: Ten pence

Amazing story of police raid on the 'luncheon voucher' brothel

THE PEER, THE VICARS AND SEX FOR SALE

THE HOUSE in Streatham raided by police — among "guests," a peer and several vicars.

MEMBER of the House of ds, several vicars and an MP n Ireland were among 53 men

Standard Reporter

Today at the Inner London Crown Court, the brothel keeper, 47-year-old Cynthia Payne, was jailed for 18 months, fined £650 on each of three charges of exercising control over prostitutes and ordered to pay legal costs not exceeding £2000. She

"When police went upstairs they found men and women in pairs who were queueing outside the bedrooms.

"There were sparsely-dressed women running in and out of the hall. In each room police found one or more couples having sexual intercourse or having

12. Headline on the day of the trial.

13. The Squadron Leader exuding Eastern promise.

14. Accommodating the bank manager.

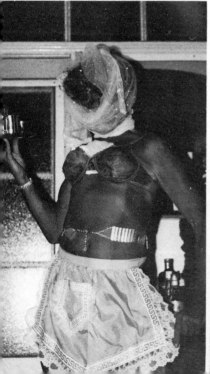

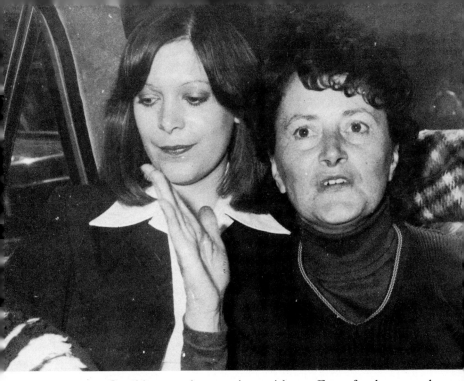

15. Cynthia returning to prison with an officer after her appeal.

16. Mitchell, the Squadron Leader, exercising Cynthia's other dog outside Holloway Prison.

17. Cynthia (*left*) being greeted on her release from prison by Selma James.

yourself then, Dominic?" I said before he could even get through the door. "Oh yes, Mum," he said, with a smile on his face. I was over the bloody moon, I was so pleased.'

Dominic saw his father on rare occasions in the course of his childhood. He did not like what he saw. He made it clear to Cynthia that he could live as easily without Terence as Terence had lived without him. Terence did not receive an invitation to his son's wedding.

'I told Terry that Dominic was going to be married. He was upset that he hadn't been asked to the ceremony.'

He saw something of it, though. Terence watched his son and daughter-in-law as they posed for photographs on the steps of the church: he was some distance away, on the opposite side of the street. He could have been any idle bystander for all Dominic knew. After the newly-weds and their guests had driven off to the reception, Terence returned to the seaside town where he had had such fun with the volatile seventeen-year-old who later bore him the child whom he hoped would be possessed of his own intelligence.

Cynthia adopted several aliases while she was working as a prostitute. For some time she wavered between Heather Rumbold and Judith Mansell. As Judith Mansell-Smith she deemed herself a business consultant and had the occupation printed on her notepaper. 'That Mansell-Smith was a bit of a disaster really. There was more than one bloke who assumed that because I had a double-barrelled handle I must be posh. They expected a duchess type with a cut-glass voice, and then they saw me. "You're not quite what I had in mind," a well-dressed gentleman said – he'd only heard me say "Hullo". He scarpered down the stairs like greased bloody lightning.'

Cynthia's flat in west London was raided by the police, following a complaint from someone living in the same block. She pleaded guilty to the charge of keeping a brothel, even though Dolores was only engaged to answer the telephone and see the men on and off the premises. The presence of another woman, albeit a comparatively innocent one, was enough to make the charge stick. Cynthia decided to settle for a quick fine rather than contest the case. She needed to get back to work.

Unfortunately for the two women, the brief session in the magistrates' court was referred to in several newspapers. Dolores's family were horrified to read that a girl they had always considered totally respectable had been convicted for prostitution. Despite her assurances that she had only acted as Cynthia's maid, they continued to express their shock and outrage. The fact that she worked in a sinful establishment was wicked enough in their eyes. Their behaviour did nothing to convince Dolores that the ways of this world are just. She sank into a deeper gloom, if that was possible.

She tendered her resignation to Cynthia, who tried to persuade her to stay. 'It was no use. She was really bitter about the fine and being labelled a prostitute. Her family gave her a rough time. I understood how she felt. She was bloody terrified of a second arrest, now that she was known to the police.'

Cynthia was not long in finding someone to replace Dolores. Her successor, Janet, was much more a woman of the world. Janet had been on the game herself for fifteen arduous years, and had given it up after succumbing to a nervous breakdown. She specialized in 'kinky bondage fellows' – barristers, Members of Parliament, stockbrokers and assorted businessmen. She was the ideal maid for Cynthia in that she could detect a potentially dangerous or awkward customer simply by looking at him.

It was through Janet that Cynthia met Gregory, who has exerted a lasting influence on her. Gregory had been one of Janet's strangest clients: on his first visit to her flat in Paddington, he had brought with him a special chair which he had designed and built. Janet was required to secure him into this 'punishment chair' by means of various straps and to leave him in it for an indefinite period. There was no sexual contact whatsoever: merely to be tied and bolted into his own variation of the stocks was all that was needed to ensure Gregory's complete satisfaction.

Janet felt sorry for Gregory and developed a friendship

with him. In this he was uniquely privileged because Janet had kept all her other punters at a professional distance: they were known to her solely as a series of peculiar demands. Janet was struck by Gregory's sensitive nature and later by his wide-ranging intelligence. She welcomed him into her small circle of acquaintances. Cynthia was as impressed by Gregory as he was by her. 'It was funny, but I knew I could help him in some way, just as he could help me. I hadn't been working on him for very long before he put that bloody punishment chair up in the attic. "What you want from life goes deeper than that," I told him. I was bloody right, too. I think I gave him the courage to face the truth about himself – that he's only happy when he's dressed as a woman. As for him, he taught me a hell of a lot about domination and how to keep a slave under control. It's thanks to Greg and to dear old Mitch, the Squadron Leader, that I came out of myself and started to enjoy life again. Plenty of men have known my body, but it's only Gregory who knows my mind.'

In the summer of 1972 Cynthia persuaded Roger to drive her to Margate.

'I went to Dreamland Park and there was Sam, just as he'd used to be, behind the ball game. I hadn't been down there for ten years and I didn't really expect to see him and I just looked behind the ball game and there he was. It was quite amazing, actually, that twelve years had gone past – I can still see the look of astonishment on his face, because he was thinking back to the time when he called me over to his ball game. There he was, and had I known I was going to meet him I'd have been all dressed up and everything. I looked bloody terrible. I'd just had this nervous breakdown over a bloody bloke, a copper called Wally, and I was in a shocking state. Anyway, I rushed over to him, and he put his arms round me and kissed and cuddled me as if ... well, you wouldn't have thought twelve years had gone past, and while he was cuddling me several people who had known me when I was a young girl, when I was his Doll, they were all watching. As he was cuddling me there was no doubt about it in my mind – there was still something there. I was a bit emotional. I said, "You've got two kids now, haven't you?" He said, "Yes. I have." And I remember saying, "Yes, but you got rid of mine, didn't you?" I remember saying something like that, I remember thinking, "I'll sling that one into your face." That made him feel rotten. He kept on cuddling me, though. "It's nice to see you, Doll," he said. And I said, "You will look in on me, won't you? Here's my 'phone number. You will 'phone me, won't you?" Sam said yes, but he never did. Then I wrote to him. "Now I want *you* to come round and see *me*" – that's what I wrote. He didn't reply. I should have gone to Margate on my own and pushed it, but at the time I couldn't – I thought he would contact me, but he didn't. When he kissed and cuddled me it was as if twelve years hadn't gone past. I felt I could easily have started the relationship all over again. I think he sensed what I was feeling. I wrote him another letter. "I know how to handle you now. I can cope with sex now." But no, he never contacted me. I think he was divorcing his wife and was frightened of getting involved with me. He was the only man I ever wanted to marry.'

7

'Old men are more appreciative'

Cynthia was so careful with the money she earned as a prostitute that she eventually amassed enough to buy a small terrace house in Edencourt Road, Streatham.

'It was a poky little place compared to what I've got now, but at least it was a proper home. I had my own bricks and mortar at long last. I was beginning to see my dream of security come true. I still had a rented flat in the West End, and it was in there that I started my brothel activities – on a small scale, naturally. I had to be a bit cautious when I moved to Streatham. I had to find out the lie of the land. I didn't want the neighbours suspecting anything; I didn't want them to know what I was up to. I wanted to pass myself off as respectable.'

She succeeded in her ambition. It wasn't until the police raid on Cranmore in December 1978, and the interest it attracted in the national newspapers, that the residents of Edencourt Road became aware of what kind of householder had once lived among them.

'They never had a bloody clue, I was that discreet. I used to give my sex parties at lunch time, when the other woman in the road were busy in their kitchens. I spaced them out to start with and then I gave one every other month, regular like. I told the people living on either side of me that I liked to hold a business conference, seeing as how I was a consultant, on a friendly basis – it was surprising, I told them, how much work you could get done over a drink and a ham or cheese roll, with some nice music playing in the background. Some of my gentlemen owned really swish motors, Rolls-Royces and such, so I gave them strict instructions not to park them in Edencourt Road: "You just leave that bloody Jaguar round the corner," I'd say. "It may be beautiful, but it's far too posh for a street like this. It draws attention to the house." I had to be a bully to protect myself. Most of the blokes were sensible when it came to parking, though – they realized the trouble I could have had with the neighbours if Edencourt Road was crammed chock-a-block with strangers' cars taking up the residents' parking space. I kept in with the Irish family next door by giving them the left-overs from my parties – cold chicken, if there was any, and the odd roll or two. They weren't well-off, so the food went down a fair treat with them. They really believed I was a businesswoman. I was, of course, but not in the way they thought. Oh, I was in my element.'

The sex parties were not a new venture for Cynthia. By the time she settled in Streatham, she was already an experienced hostess.

'I love entertaining. It's my greatest pleasure in life. It was years before I came up with the idea of an admission charge, and even then it was only because a client put it in my mind. "You're bloody daft, Cindy," he said, "letting them have all this for nothing." He was right. In those days, I was always out of pocket after a party. Everything was free: the booze, the grub, and the fucking. I'd laid it all on, just for the fun of it. It never bloody occurred to me that I could enjoy myself *and* make a profit at the same time. I had some real riff-raff at the early parties. They soon got the push. I don't cater for young men any more, unless they're transvestites or slaves, or both. Blokes under forty are all Jack-my-lads, who think their pricks are bloody priceless. They like to boast, and boasting's something I can't be doing with in men or in woman.

'Anyway, I discovered the secret of how to organize a marvellous sex party – find the willing girls, supply a lesbian display, and get enough older men who'll be grateful for the sex they're paying for. Give them plenty to eat and drink. That was always my biggest problem – finding the willing girls. I'll never forget, I put a special advertisement in one of the contact magazines: "Kinky people wanted for kinky parties." It was through that that I met Agatha and Joanna. Aggie's as plain as a bloody pikestaff, but she's a wonderful little worker in the bedroom. Her husband, Reggie, used to come to the parties with her, and he didn't give a monkey's when she went upstairs with another man. Quite the opposite – he bloody smiled. "She's a bundle of energy, my missus" –that's what he'd say. I've known Agatha take on three men at once – it wore you out just to watch her. I don't think there's a hole in her body that hasn't been filled. Yet if you saw her in her haberdashery shop, selling pins and needles and bibs and bobs, looking all bloody demure, you wouldn't reckon on her as a raver. We had a retired police superintendent at one party, I remember, who was really excited by her. They went upstairs and he asked Agatha to whip him. "I don't think I could," she said. "It's not something I've ever done." "There's always a first time," he said, and he was bloody pleading with her by now. Well, Agatha started to give him a good hiding, and she told me afterwards that a change came over her. Once she got into the swing of it, she couldn't bloody stop herself. She liked having a man submissible to her. "I thought of all those years washing my husband's socks and underpants, cooking his meals, waiting on him hand and foot, and it suddenly gave me a lovely feeling, punishing that policeman."'

The ex-superintendent enjoyed himself, too. He asked Agatha if he could visit her at home and do some really menial work for her. She told him that she and Reggie lived in Somerset, but that didn't put him off.

"'I *would* like my gas cooker cleaned," she said. "It hasn't been done in ten years." Would you believe it? That copper drove down to Somerset early one morning, took all his clothes off and set to on the cooker. Agatha's kitchen is just behind the shop, so it's not what you'd call private during shopping hours. Agatha had to leave Reggie on the counter while she gave the copper a few lashes. "What on earth is going on in your kitchen, Mr Pratt?" one old lady asked Reggie. "It sounds as if someone's being murdered." She didn't know how near the truth she was. The copper was screaming his head off with pleasure as the change came over Agatha – she was whipping the bloody life out of him. "I expect it's something on the television," Reggie said to the old lady. "Nothing but violence on the box these days." Oh, I have to laugh when I think about it. Agatha looks so bloody prim and proper on the surface, but she's a right demon for sex underneath. And the funny thing is, she didn't begin to lose her inhibitions until she was in her mid-forties. "I was the butter-wouldn't-melt-in-her-mouth type," she says. Well, she's had more than butter in her mouth since then. There's no stopping Agatha when she's in the mood. A strange look comes into her eyes – I call it the warning signal. If there's a bloke in the room when she gets that look, he has to surrender, he's got no bloody choice. He's a marked man.'

Joanna shares Agatha's enthusiasm, but not her resourcefulness.

'She was my other star in the days when I didn't charge. Between them, Joanna and Agatha could keep any number of men happy. Joanna never took on three at a time, but she was a wonderful worker in the bedroom. She used to be a school teacher. She's a very educated woman. She was a bit like Agatha – she realized when she was middle-aged that there was something missing from her life. She was happily married, too, but she wanted to spread herself, like. She certainly did that at Edencourt Road. She and Agatha both say that the parties went off as soon as I made the men pay for their sex, but I don't agree. I think they became a touch classier, if anything. I'll never forget, I remember saying to Joanna and Agatha, "Look, you can still have your fun, but you'll be getting some pin money as well. There aren't many people in this world who get paid for enjoying themselves." Agatha stayed on, but Joanna faded away. I sent her a few chaps who didn't mind the journey to Pulborough – she liked to do a little entertaining at home. Her husband's the same as Reggie:

94

he just toddles off to another room when a bloke comes round for a fuck. Joanna had a beautiful affair with a bloke in his early twenties, that's less than half her age. He's just got married, but he says he owes everything to Joanna – she taught him how to be a good lover. I wish more young blokes would fall for older woman. They wouldn't be such bloody Jack-my-lads then. They wouldn't be in such a hurry to get rid of their spunk. They'd learn that a woman likes to take her time – she doesn't want the bloody thing shoved in one minute and pulled out the next. I met too many men with that attitude when I was on the game, and I would never allow them in any brothel of mine.'

Cynthia was always anxious on the night before a party.

'I couldn't sleep. I was terribly excited, looking forward to all the fun. And I'd be worried, too: would my lesbians turn up? Would there be enough girls? I didn't have to worry about the men: they'd be around for a bit of the other even if it meant struggling through a bloody snowstorm. I learned early in life with Terry that if you tell a man you're going to drop your drawers for him, he'll fight his way through fire and bloody flood to get to you. There was one party, I remember, when dozens of blokes arrived, but not a single girl. Every time the doorbell rang I prayed that there was a woman on the step. Those blokes stood about in my small front room like a load of dummies. I was spare, I really was. They were getting tanked up and a bit irritable, because the first thing a man wants when he goes to a sex party is to get himself despunked, it stands to reason. Then, thank God, just as I was seriously thinking that I'd have to give the men their money back, a whole troop of girls suddenly appeared out of the blue. My word, were they soon in business! The blokes were fairly panting for them. That party looked as if it would be a disaster but it turned out a great success.'

The house in Edencourt Road was kept spotlessly clean, but not by Cynthia. Her new friends, Gregory and Mitchell ('Mitch'), attended to the washing-up, the dusting and the polishing. Following one of many advertisements she placed in the various contact magazines to which she was by now subscribing, Cynthia acquired the services of Slave Rodney, who tended the tiny garden every weekend and made himself useful in a hundred ways.

'Rodney's a perfect slave. He would do anything for me. I was frightened of losing him to begin with. I'm a bossy little bugger, but I'm not a natural mistress. I had to take lessons from Gregory on how to keep a slave happily humiliated. I suppose it's because I've got a bit of the actress in my nature that I was able to pretend to be nasty. Some woman are right cows and don't have to put on a show, but not me. It's quite a strain sometimes, being thoroughly bloody unpleasant to sweet and gentle blokes like Slave Rodney and Slave Philip. I hate to hear myself saying the things I have to say to them, but they love the insults, they can't get enough of them. It's not easy, trying to find fault with their work – you couldn't have a better gardener than Slave Rodney, and Slave Philip's painting and decorating is bloody wonderful, it really is.'

Slave Philip was taken on by Cynthia when she moved to Cranmore, by which time she had accumulated a large band of 'licensed jesters', as she describes her clients, her girls, and her contentedly submissive servants.

Cynthia was at last in her element, giving her monthly parties and presiding over her 'brothel days', each Tuesday and Friday.

'You have to appreciate that there are a lot of gentlemen who wouldn't be seen dead at a party. It's not just that some of them are famous and don't want to be recognized, it's because they like their sex to be private. The kinky bondage fellows don't object to a party so long as it's on a small scale, but then the other guests have to be kinky too. I used to enjoy organizing those – they really challenged my imagination. Janet offered me plenty of good advice, with all her experience of strict discipline. I had this really beautiful girl who looked bloody wonderful in leather – old Mitch would get really carried away, grovelling at her feet. No kinky do was complete without Magda. The kinkiest parties I gave were planned around a bank manager. He was difficult to satisfy at first because no amount of humiliation was good enough for him – he wanted more, more, more. Magda would whip him after Mitch had tied him up, but still he wasn't happy. "I want mud, Madam," he said to me one day. "Where the bloody hell do you think I'm going to get mud from?" I shouted at him. "I'm not traipsing off to the seaside just for you."

'Anyway, I gave his request some thought. A madam who takes her work seriously has to consider her customers' requirements. I was listening to Gregory cleaning one of the carpets with the Hoover when I had a flash of inspiration. I 'phoned the bank manager straight away. "Be at the flat on Friday" – I was using the flat as a brothel still – "I've found the very thing for you." I was terribly excited. I could hardly wait for Friday to come round. I ordered Gregory to clean the house from top to bottom, because I wanted the Hoover bag to be full to bursting. I'll never forget setting off for the bus stop with a Hoover bag in my hold-all. That bus journey to the West End seemed to take for ever. When I got to the flat, I told Magda and Mitch what I intended to do. It had to be a surprise for the bank manager. When he arrived, he was commanded to undress. We covered his naked body with baby oil and then we strung him up. I opened the Hoover bag and the three of us pelted him with the muck inside. He was in his seventh heaven. Some of the stuff stuck to him, which was exactly what he wanted. He looked bloody horrible by the time we'd finished with him, like a monster from the deep. He thanked me after we cut him down. "That was a brainwave of yours," he said. I called him a disgusting sod and ordered him to wash. That clinched it. He was squirming with pleasure.'

Cynthia never lost contact with her family, though relations between her and her father and sister were often strained. Melanie, in particular, expressed contempt when she learned about Cynthia's chosen occupation. One memorable evening, Cynthia, Gregory and Mitch had dinner with Melanie and Kevin at their house on the outskirts of a Sussex resort. The meal was a success, and the conversation amicable. When it was time to leave, Cynthia revealed that her sister and brother-in-law had just been entertaining a couple of transvestites.

'Kevin was furious,' Melanie told me. 'He was under the impression that Mitch and Gregory were both normal, ordinary, decent men. They behaved themselves at our table, that's true – but to learn as they were going that they dressed up as women! Kevin was horrified that the news would get round the town that he had had a pair of deviants in his house. I could cheerfully strangle my sister when she does things like that.'

A truly startling change was effected in Cynthia's uneasy and frequently quarrelsome relationship with her father – a distinct change for the better, in her view. As Hamilton grew older and lonelier, he became increasingly frustrated. He closed down his business and consequently had little to occupy him. He was well aware that his eldest child was now the proud owner of a brothel, in an area not commonly associated with immorality, though he didn't pass on this information to his fellow Freemasons: pillars of the community don't have madams as daughters. He kept the knowledge to himself, but he made use of it nevertheless.

'Dad turned up one night on my doorstep, really far gone in his cups. He could hardly stand up, he was so bloody squiffy. I let him in, and I said, "For Christ's sake, Dad, what are you doing in London this late?" It was after midnight. "I want a girl," he said. "You're drunk," I said. "Get me a girl, Cinders. You know how." I kept on telling him he was drunk; it was the whisky speaking, I told him. "You go to bed and sleep it off and we'll hear what you have to say in the morning." I was convinced that he would be thoroughly ashamed of himself when he woke up, he was that kind of man. Either that, or he'd forget that he ever asked me. Anyway, he came into my bedroom the following day and he said to me, "Cinders, I meant every word of what I said to you last night." I was bloody flabbergasted. He was stone cold sober by now – it wasn't a drunkard talking any more. "I want you to find me a woman. You specialize in looking after the needs of older men – well, Cinders, I'm an older man, and I need a woman." I played it cool, even though I was bloody thunderstruck – he was the last person in this world I would have expected to ask me for a girl. I mean, he was my own bloody father. "Listen, Dad, you'll have to give me time to think this over. It's come as a bit of a shock to me." Then he said, "Don't take too long about it, there's a good Cinders." I'll never forget, I'd never known him to be so bloody nice to me. Typical man, I thought – all smarm when he wants his oats. "You've got to understand, Dad," I said, "that it's my policy to find the right girl for the right bloke. It's hard work sometimes, because some people just don't make a match. I'll do my best for you."

'He went back home, and I was still wondering whether he was serious. I was in two minds about the whole business. It wasn't as if he'd helped me when I was desperate, and I had been desperate more than once, and he bloody knew it. What happened was, I decided to do as he wanted. I've never been one to harbour grudges. You can waste your life that way. I sat down and thought about getting him a girl and then I had one of my brainwaves. I remembered Mavis, who'd been Melanie's best friend at school. She'd worked for Dad for a while and he told me he'd fancied her something rotten. He didn't know that while she was working for him she was having it away with every single one of his trainee barbers. He wanted to make a pass at her, but he thought that because she was so ladylike she might take offence. And he didn't have a bloody clue, and no more did Melanie, that when he came and asked me to organize a bit of the other for him that Mavis was one of my girls. I've sent dozens of blokes to Mavis and they've all come back raving about her. She's a genuine French polisher, the real McCoy. She gives the most bloody wonderful blow-job it's possible to have. She's an artist at it. Mavis – or Thelma, as a lot of her clients know her – is a very warm-hearted person, very considerate and kind. She's another one with an understanding husband. Bert always takes the dog for a walk when a bloke turns up for a gam. He realizes that the £15 she charges comes in handy, but he appreciates that Mavis has to express herself, and that's the way she likes to do it. They've got the perfect marriage. The only time in the year that Mavis doesn't work is when her daughter is home for the holidays from university.

'Anyhow, my brainwave was to fix my father up with Mavis. I rang her up and asked if she was agreeable. We both had a bloody good laugh, and she said yes. So then I 'phoned Dad and I said, "Dad, I've got just the right girl for you. She doesn't live very far from you. Here's her address and telephone number. When you ring, ask to speak to Thelma." I was splitting my bloody sides when I hung up. I was terribly excited, I'll never forget, waiting to hear from either one of them how it all went. Dad arrived at Mavis's place and he had no idea that he'd be getting a gam from the well-spoken friend of Melanie who'd worked for him when she was a teenager. He nearly keeled over with surprise when Mavis opened the front door. "Come in, Mr Payne," she said. "Or can I call you Hamilton?" He couldn't believe his bloody eyes. He went into the house and Mavis made him a nice cup of tea and then she gave him a sample of her French polishing. He'd never known anything like it in his life before.'

Thus it was that Hamilton Payne joined his daughter's happy band of 'licensed jesters'.

'He never missed a party if he could help it. The first time he watched a lesbian display his eyes were out on stalks, he was so bloody amazed. He became much more broadminded in the last years of his life. He'd always been very prejudiced, very Victorian, about anything to do with sex, and there he was looking at two girls making love on the floor of my lounge and thoroughly enjoying himself. There was one bloody wonderful evening when he said to me, "Cinders, I really fancy that gorgeous bird who's just walked in." Well, the gorgeous bird was a bloke in drag. "You won't have any luck there, Dad," I said. "She's a he." He was knocked sideways. "And what's more," I said, "he's dead normal even though he's dressed as a woman." That flummoxed him, I can tell you. It took hours trying to convince him that very few transvestites are gay – or queer, which was the horrible bloody word he always used. He couldn't make it out. "If a man wants to get into woman's clothes then he must be a cissy" – that was his line. Gregory and me, we told him otherwise.

'Dad soon came to see what a sheltered life he'd had and how much more I knew than he did about a lot of things. I can honestly say that I taught him to be tolerant. It was about bloody time, as far as I was concerned. I used to have this lovely transsexual at my parties – Martin, his name was then; now that he's had the operation and made the change, she's Martina. It was a bloody wonderful moment when Dad took Martin on his lap and gave him a little cuddle. He wasn't the tyrant of my childhood at all – I was looking at a nice old man instead of the so-and-so I'd argued with for years on end. Dad really entered into the spirit of my parties. He didn't blink an eye after a while when Mitch came in in his bra and panties, wearing his yashmak and showing off his stocking tops. He wasn't a bit put out when Gregory served breakfast dressed as the maid. Oh, I used to enjoy kidding him. "What would Melanie say if she knew you were here?" "You won't tell her, will you, Cinders?" "That depends."

'I'll never forget, he turned into the father I'd always wanted him to be, except that it was too bloody late now. He hadn't lifted a finger when I touched rock bottom and was crying out for affection. He was too taken up with his business to be bothered with his own flesh and blood. He'd washed his hands of me once too often. Still, for all that, I couldn't turn my back on him. It upset me to think of him pining away on his own when he could be mixing with other old boys and having lots of fun.'

Hamilton 'went upstairs' at Cranmore on numerous occasions.

'My lovely Indian girl, Karmala, was his favourite. He confessed things to her that he never said to me. He told her what a lousy father he'd been, and how he was trying to make up for all the damage he'd done. She's a bloody wonderful listener, Karmala, and she let him talk to his heart's content. That's what some blokes want – the chance to talk. I know that's what my father wanted, apart from sex, of course.

'I'll never forget, it was on one of his last visits to the house, Karmala was working overtime trying to get him roused. He got in a terrible state because he couldn't keep it up. I mean, he had trouble staying hard. He was practically in tears. Karmala asked me what she ought to do. I suggested a vibrator, but she didn't know how to work it. I went with her into the bedroom and I plugged in the vibrator and showed Karmala how to stroke it up and down Dad's cock. I was too embarrassed to put it on Dad myself – I demonstrated in the air, if you get my meaning. After all, he was my father. "Have you got the hang of it, Karmala?" I asked, hoping like hell that she had. I watched for a minute or two while she copied what I'd done and then I left them to it. I think it wounded his pride, the fact that Karmala had to use a vibrator. "Needs must ... " and all that. It was a sad experience for him, but no sadder than what hundreds of other old blokes have to go through. That was what my brothel was for – to give the elderly their confidence back. If one of my girls lost patience with a client, I would have to know why. There had to be a bloody good reason. Sometimes I took the girl's side, especially if a bloke was getting stroppy and blaming her for something he couldn't manage himself. Other times, though, I reminded the girl that my house wasn't just any house, and that there were certain little things you could do for a grandad that a young man wouldn't appreciate. Nine times out of ten, the girls would stick to my rules and play fair. It was only the odd newcomer who caused trouble, and that was usually because she was nervous and probably a bit tiddly as a result. Anyway, when all else fails, plug in the vibrator. It certainly did the trick for Dad.'

Hamilton Payne died in 1979, shortly before Cynthia stood trial for running a brothel and keeping a disorderly house.

'I was glad he was spared the publicity; the disgrace of knowing that his eldest daughter had been sent to prison. He wouldn't have been able to look people in the eye if he'd gone on living. That was one small mercy. I like to think that I made him happy towards the end. The two of us became as close as we ever could be, given his behaviour in the past. He let me open my heart to him, and I did, I told him about every single bloody grievance. I'll never forget, he gave me some sensible advice once. He'd heard me bawling at Dom-

inic and he said to me, "Cinders, don't make the same mistake
with Dominic that I made with you. I used to explode, when
I should have tried to reason with you. We're both impatient,
you and me. You don't want Dominic to feel for you what
you felt for me all those years." He was right, of course. He
recognized himself in my attitude. He could see where he'd
gone wrong. It was a pity he hadn't seen it earlier. As I say,
he was a very different Hamilton Payne when he was at my
parties from the tyrant who did his darndest to keep me
down.

'Oh, we had some bloody wonderful laughs together. I told
him the truth about Terry and the garden shed and he nearly
bust a gut, he found it so funny. He was a nice old boy at the
end because he was having it off whenever he felt like it. It
just goes to prove what I've always maintained – that men
are much more pleasant and considerate so long as they're
regularly despunked. If they're not getting their oats, they're
bloody pests. It took Dad a lot of courage as well as a lot of
whisky to ask me to provide him with a girl, and I have to say
that he never regretted it. There aren't many daughters who
have done what I've done for their fathers. I still chuckle
when I think that Hamilton Payne was one of my most
satisfied customers.'

Melanie did not, and does not, chuckle at the thought: 'He
could have behaved with a bit more dignity. If there was one
word he drummed into our ears when we were children, that
word was "respectable". Well, I don't call going to bed with
your youngest daughter's best friend "respectable". I can't
bear to speak to Mavis now. I was, frankly, appalled when
my sister told me the sordid details. She laughed, of course.'

A post mortem revealed that Hamilton's death was due to
cirrhosis of the liver.

'The funny thing was, he'd been warned about his heart –
so he gave up smoking. He was like a bloody furnace for most
of his life: he must have been lighting up sixty a day at least.
But I don't think there was a doctor alive who could have
persuaded him to stop drinking. My Dad was a real pub man.
He loved to prop up the saloon bar of a Saturday night. He
started on the booze when he was on the ships and I doubt if

he ever came off it until his dying day. He was seventy-five, which isn't a bad age for a heavy drinker.'

Hamilton's estate was divided between his daughters. At Cynthia's insistence, he left £500 to 'Jersey Lil': 'I told him it was the least he could do. She brought him a lot of pleasure when he needed it most. As a token of gratitude, I said.'

Cynthia was surprised, and touched, to discover that her far from doting father had kept all her letters to him, and even those she wrote to Melanie. In one of these, written when she was five months pregnant with Dominic, she tries to reassure Hamilton that one of his daughters will give him cause for pride:

Thank Melanie for the frocks I'm grateful really for them also I appreciate for what your doing for me I dont show it I know but I think all the more. I understand any parent being dissapointed but these things happen and nothing can stop them. Its a lot of my mind really now that you know I was quite prepared to wait until I'd had the child, but I suppose that would have been a worse shock. It would have saved you worrying all this time. I've always have been a worry and I expect I always will dont expect I'll ever change and its never done intentionally funny enough I always seem to sail into it. And Melanie is the appostite she's always been good no trouble at all for her shes a lovely kid really something to be proud of there but you dont seem to think she's all that wonderful really do you? You probably dont notice it being at home with her all the time. She's got poise now and she's cultered in her speech one would think she's had a very good education to study her well sometimes. The dreams that you had for me Melanie will do just fine she'll always do well for herself no need for anxiety there. Sorry it had to be that way for you. Ever since I was a little girl I always told myself one day I'll be just right for you that I'd try to make an improvement but no I try but it just dont happen. Still there's a good many years yet to come for me to make up to you. Cant see anything in your letter why I should send it back to you still I'll do it just the same. I went to the Clinic last night

took Blood Pressure and different things I'm alright so far.
I just get a bit tired at work at the end of the day with my
feet but me I'm always tired specially at work so I dont
think that can be any excuse *ha ha*

Goodnight for now

All my love

Cinders xx

Among Hamilton's papers, too, was a curiously nasty mis-
sive, set down in handwriting similar to that of Jack the
Ripper:

Mr Payne/
    Sir your daughter stayed the night with a married man
at Brighton on Monday 1st of May they stayed in Queens
Rd. in a Hotel, Cynthia told me I told my Mam, she said
I should tell You the man is Terry lives with Vincent
Browns mother I thought I should tell you, because it is
wrong and there might be trouble. Yours truly

L. Monday

'Bloody little sneak. I never knew she'd written to him. It
gave me quite a shock, finding that in his desk. It's a mystery,
it really is, the things people keep.'

It became clear to Cynthia that the house in Edencourt Road
was too small to accommodate her ever expanding clientèle. A
large, rambling, Victorian mansion was what she needed.
    With Mitch's financial assistance, she acquired Cranmore.
    'I couldn't have bought it without his loan. Thank God he
had faith in me. I'll never forget, I said to him, "Now I can
run the brothel of my dreams." I fell in love with the place
instantly. I went from room to room, thinking to myself what
bloody wonderful parties I'd be able to give. In the summer,
the clients could take their drinks into the garden; oh, it
would be so civilized after the cramped conditions I was used
to working in. I was terribly excited at the thought of running
a knocking shop in that posh suburban street.'

By the time she moved into Cranmore, Cynthia had already established the particular kind of brothel she was happiest supervising.

'I've always been fond of the elderly. I came to the conclusion that my brothel was going to cater for the needs of old men. I didn't rule out younger blokes, but I set the minimum age at forty. I decided to charge reasonable prices, because some of my clients had little more than their pensions to live on. I used to give a special £3 discount to old age pensioners. I left it to my wealthier clients to pay what they felt like paying – that way they were subsidizing the poorer blokes. My girls all agree that old men are more appreciative. They show courtesy, and of course they don't make excessive demands when they're in their seventies and eighties. Oh, we had a bloody wonderful atmosphere going before the raid stopped everything. Just to see an old boy come down the stairs with a smile on his face – even if he was a bit puffed out – used to give me a glow, it really did. I would fix him some poached eggs on toast and make him a nice cup of tea or a mug of beef extract and I'd sit on the other side of the kitchen table and chat to him until he got his energy back. There aren't many brothels that offer that kind of service.'

The 'bloody wonderful atmosphere' was disrupted on December 6th, 1978. It was recreated on one occasion, in July 1981, in special circumstances.

INTERLUDE

'A miniature atomic explosion'

Box D 434,
Dear Madam,
I would like to attend your next party if I am acceptable. I am male, aged 44, fit and strong, a former cavalryman, weight stripped 10 stones 7 lbs. Height 5′ 8½″ Chest 38 Waist 30, good shapely buttocks.

I was used as an exhibit at a party about twelve months ago in London. Two of the highlights were when my body was used for a treasure hunt by the guests who could buy 5 pins for 2/6 to stick in and try and find the treasure. The spot was picked by the hostess. The winner took all the money as the prize.

Secondly at midnight with all the lights out and in pitch darkness two young ladies lit my pubic hair with matches burning it all off. Further details can be supplied, if you are interested.

Yours
Exhibitionist Piers

Dear Judith,
May I make my visit on Friday 17th. You ask what I want you to do with the boxing gloves well to tell you the truth it

107

was my intention that I repeated what I did last time and that you just put the gloves on.

However as you have now increased your fee I'm not sure quite if you had anything in mind, you mention if I would like you to punch me on the nose and I feel that I could stand the treatment it sounds rather exciting. Did you mean this and would you like to do this to me?

You see Judith I have been very interested in women boxing and wrestling for some years and I have a rather large collection of photographs on this subject, and I was wondering if you should know of anywhere in town that holds such functions.

Please write by return I am enclosing stamp.

Dear Bizarre Lady,

Have just read my first copy of New Friends, and was delighted to find your advt. I have been interested in way-out fun ever since my divorce two years ago, but find answering shop window postcards most disappointing. Maybe you have something better to offer?

I am 46 years of age, 6 feet tall, weight 12 stone and have fair hair, blue eyes. Am well endowed with the symbol of manhood, uncircumcised, but with very free moving foreskin due to exercise!! Am strong and virile and experienced in many ways.

Have taken part in bondage incidents, and shared pleasure with as many as three other people at once.

Should like to come and visit you with a view to submitting to any form of verbal/physical examination of my interests/abilities, and would do all I could to demonstrate that I was the right person to come to your parties.

Do please write soon and fix me up. My longing is growing with every word I write, my buttocks ache for the sting of your riding whip.

Dear Advertiser,

Very interested in your advertisement. I am aged 45 and

desperate for some unhurried attention. Would you be prepared to wear a shirt and tie (supplied if necessary) during
treatment? Please give full details of service offered including
fees.

P.S. Presumably bondage is included.

Dear Lady Y. 19,
   I am seeking a new Mistress and your ad has prompted me
to ask whether or not I will be accepted as a regular visitor,
That is, if you are wicked enough to treat me as I deserve,
and as my former Mistress used me, She has, due to her
husbands business, moved to Suffolk and it is no longer
practical to travel so far, hence my looking for a Lady nearer
home, I am going to be perfectly frank and honest with you,
and tell you what treatment I enjoyed, and what 'gift' I am
prepared to give you for a Regular fortnightly session, If
none of my suggestions appeal to you just answer 'No', and
it will be quite O.K.
   When we are undressed, my Mistress shows her respect
for me by spitting in my face. I take along my own Handcuffs
and key for her, I am then made helpless and gagged with a
pair of her soiled panties, when I am in this position, She
then amuses herself with me in various ways, most of them
painful to me, She is quite proficient with her whip and cane,
She also makes good use of her Finger nails, Teeth, Feet and
has even used her cigarette on me while sitting suffocatingly
on my face, thus preventing any objections or crying out from
me. She always uses those words that are normally 'taboo'.
                           Hoping to hear from You.

My dear Lady,
   I reply to your advertising H. 39. and I wish very frankly
to meet with you, for a afternoon frolics. I love you, to, as
you say, dominant to me.
   I love very much yours dimensions, you must be a lovely
and charming lady where every body love to be with.

I enclose a remitance, I think will be enough to let me have you photo.

I am looking forward for you.

sincerily

X Ari xxxxxxxxxxxxxxx

with my love

Dear Judith,

Judith, you are the only person I know who is genuinely understanding and well-organised, so I am writing to you very frankly to ask if you can please help me, and if you can possibly put me in touch with the right person, I would not, of course, remain ungrateful.

Ideally, I am seeking one, regular, understanding lady friend, whom I could visit every two months for an hour or so, preferably between 1–3 pm (Mon–Thurs.) although I might arrange a morning visit, if more convenient to her. Frankly, I prefer someone rather older, aged 38 to 46 if possible, and preferably English (including Jewish), otherwise European, blonde or brunette ... perhaps a frustrated housewife? Her appearance is entirely unimportant to my way of thinking. She can be plain, thin, scruffy, etc ... or buxom or matronly (like, for example, the maid in your flat ... with the foreign accent ... I don't suppose, though, she is one of your team?) ... but what is *really* important (and I do mean this *very* sincerely) is that she should have a *very* strong, *natural* odour coming through her blouse from under her arms, as this is the only thing that turns me on about a woman more than anything else, I promise you. I myself am, of course, spotlessly clean.

That is to say, when I arrive, she should be dressed in a knee-length woollen, nylon, polyester or tricel dress, blouse/skirt or blouse/slax (black, if poss., but this is not important) and for at least 2 days and nights beforehand she will not have washed once under her arms, or used any artificial disguises such as perfume, eau de cologne, deodorants, powder, etc., so that she has a very noticeable sweaty 'pong' coming through her blouse. This would really mean everything to me, and I would then like to undress her slowly, giving her 'O' under each arm, while she played with me, etc. It is also very important that the clothes do not have the slightest trace of any scent or deodorant that she may normally have used beforehand.

If it would be more convenient to her, I could see her perhaps on a Monday, so that she could go the whole weekend without washing, and thus would not embarrass her other friends. To produce the right effect, she could have a bath on the Friday night, but using 'simple' or non-perfumed household soap (Fairy), then put on a clean set of clothes or undies. She would then not wash or once remove her blouse until we met on the Monday, even sleeping in it each night ... and nature would do the rest.

My request is really quite a simple one and not really all that demanding, if you consider that less than 100 years ago, when ladies seldom took a bath and scent was too costly for most people to afford, it was considered perfectly normal for ladies to smell of 'B.O.' under their arms. Even today, there are many ladies like that, as I know only too well, when travelling in the crowded rush-hour Tube on a hot summer's evening ... or if you visit any of the large, over-heated stores in Oxford Street towards closing time and walk behind some of the sales supervisors, you will soon see (or rather smell!) what I mean ... and you can perhaps imagine just how frustrated I feel on such occasions, as I find that odour so *very* sexy!

If you do not know of any mature lady in the age group I have mentioned, perhaps one of your younger ones may be willing to prepare herself in the way I have suggested? You are the only understanding person I know in whom I can confide, Judith, so I do hope you can help me. I could come over one afternoon and we could either have a chat, or you could perhaps even introduce me there to someone suitable?

Hope you are keeping well.

Dear Madam,

I do not know a lot about transvestites, but the idea fascinates me, and I should enjoy meeting such people, although I

do not wish to become one myself. Although I am not homosexual, I think that a really good transvestite would excite me
quite a lot – especially if he were the dominant type. With a
truly dominant woman, I am of course completely docile and
subservient, and before coming to this part of the country to
live, I spent six months as a slave in the home of a German
lady who used a very firm hand with me, and often ordered
me to my knees before her. I learned obedience in that house,
but circumstances arose which made it wiser for me to leave,
although I did not find it an easy thing to do, or probably I
should still be there. I can tell you about this in detail if we
meet. I should only tell you the plain truth – I do not like
people who imagine or invent things which have never really
happened.

Dear Miss Mansell,

You sound just the sort of person for whom I have been
searching. I have all my own clothes. These include ordinary
frocks and dresses and including a variety of girls' undies,
corsets, high heel shoes and boots, together with wigs. I have
also one or two outfits, such as a maid's and schoolgirl's
uniform and am excellent at housework. I also enjoy bondage
and moderate discipline and I like to be treated as a girl in a
lesbian relationship and be made to pay homage to my girl
friend. If you possess a dildo, so much the better, so that you
can humiliate me even further. The only thing I would ask of
you in addition would be to make me up, as this is an art that
is beyond me.

I have some leg cuffs which entail taking small steps when
walking and I could bring these too if you wished, although
I prefer to travel as light as possible.

I love to make oral devotions to a girl when dressed as a
girl myself.

Dear Judith,

It was such a pleasure to meet you briefly this evening. I
wonder if you know how much of a relief it is to speak of

something secret to someone who understands at once, and is so sympathetic into the bargain!

It was very nice to think that I might know even more than you 'what men like', and I can't resist going on a bit more about my favourite subject. I enclose a couple of pictures I took of dear Jasmin in two outfits I bought her. As you see, she is wearing a *grey* box-pleated gym tunic, specially shortened for her so as to show lots of leg when she is standing up, and of course white socks. The striped tie she found herself. We got the tunic and hat from John Lewis, the blouse from Marks and Spencer. Notice the hair ribbons and the plaits.

Knickers are a bit of a problem, because I really like them to have brief elasticated legs, but nowadays little girls wear them cut more like briefs, and there isn't real elastic in the legs. Jasmin sometimes wore small directoires which had exactly the same effect I like.

Colours are important. The knickers should *always* be a different colour from the tunic or the dress, as then they show up better. Please not black! Navy-blue are nice, and green, and of course white. I think Sonia should have all three, and perhaps change them during the session. The tunic can be grey or green, or even maroon, as navy is a bit dull.

As you see, I also got Jasmin a striped frock like they wear in the summer. We went out on Hampstead Heath and caused a sensation! You'll notice how very short it is: actually, it's pinned up at her waist, which I enjoy doing myself. These are two *very* modest pictures of her, some of the others are a bit too warm to send through the post in case they burn the envelope.

Summing it up, the outfit should be as *authentic* as possible, and it's most important that the knickers are proper schoolgirl ones and not just grown-up panties. I do so look forward to hearing from you again, and do let me know if I can help in any way to get Sonia fitted out.

Would you be very kind and return the pictures to me by using enclosed label?

Dearest Mistress

Take me and train me to be an efficient loyal slave to your whim. Make your voice the voice that initiates all my actions.

Squeeze my soul through your fingers like putty. Humiliate me. I am a slim T.V. with a passion for rubber and bondage who needs only to be shown true fear to make me into a full and dedicated slave.

Wash your feet in my tears of shame and pain.

Your Slave, 'Rhoda'.

Honoured Partygiver,

Can you supply a nun at your next shindig? Severe face and Irish accent for preference.

Yours beatifically,
'Decameron George'

Dear Advertiser,

The reasons I was attracted to your ad are that you offer CP mild – most unusual; the dominant bitchy type leave me cold. Over the past twenty years I have found that those who 'specialise' in it very often do not have any equipment for it other than a sweet pea stick and a strap off a dress, with the result that I always carry suitable items with me: lightweight tawse, plaited cat, something like a horse's tail and a paddle. Here I have half a dozen assorted canes, but they are too long to go into my suitcase, besides being awkward to carry about on the day, so would appreciate hearing what you have in this line.

Dear Miss Mansell,

I have been given your name and address by a friend who like myself is Transvestite.

I would be glad to receive details of the services you provide, and the times you are available.

As I am married with a family it is very difficult and indeed very frustrating at times to dress as I would like, and whilst my wife is reasonably sympathetic one has to think of the children, and occasionally I am in a position to pass through London on business, and this is when I get the opportunity to feel and dress as a woman.

Thanking you in anticipation.

Dear Judith,

I love lots of cuddling and kissing – a woman is a beautiful being, to be treated with care and tenderness – oh! the joy of holding and kissing her breasts, of putting my fingers between those outer lips, stimulating that magical clitoris then slipping down lower until they slide up into that warm slippery vagina-ooooooh! You can guess the condition of my penis as I write.

Dear Judith,

Thank you for your letter. I shall, if I may, call on you Wed. 8th at 6.30.

A word about myself. I'm sure you have your fill of men's troubles, but anyway.

My sex life is not at all as balanced and relaxed as it should be. I am a bachelor and have had less sex I imagine than the average man. After a deep involvement quite a few years ago I funked the whole issue and tended to take my pleasures by myself with fantasies built up from books. Quite normal sex, but fantasies.

Now I am moving back to reality (at 46!!) and find that sometimes I don't react to the real thing at all. I'm beginning to warm up slowly but it's going to be a gradual thing. A not unpleasant prospect but in the back of my mind is the little nagging feeling that my partner in the joys of sex is comparing me unfavourably with others. The sex act for me is not using the flesh of another just to get pleasure for myself; I like to be able to feel that I am giving her some pleasure and that we are co-operating in something at the heart of life and living.

Of course this may be somewhat spoilt by the realisation that the transfer of a little something from my pocket to yours is involved. But it shouldn't. At least it is perfectly honest and straightforward. You do me a big favour in return for a little one.

I'm in my forties, tall and attractive looking and have had a lot of experience in dealing with naughty girls. You can rely on me completely not to go too far, but I would be firm because that is the best way.

The spankee's bottom would be bared for a sound spanking with the slipper or strap so that she has a lovely warm backside. Other refinements I would love to discuss with you but I find these things easier on the telephone. If you would like to send your number we could have a chat and you could make sure you liked the sound of me.

In the meantime, have a very good Christmas.

Dear Miss Mansell-Smith,

I have a long, wet, active, tantalising, titillating tongue, which I can guarantee will make you writhe with pleasure and delight and when you reach your climax you will feel as if there has been a miniature atomic explosion inside of you. It is so long that I can lick the end of my nose!

I am a past Master in the Oral Arts.

P.S. To ensure complete satisfaction, I always remove my false teeth before settling down to work.

PART TWO

Her Work

18. Cynthia was driven home from prison in a client's Rolls-Royce.

19. Celebrating her restored freedom.

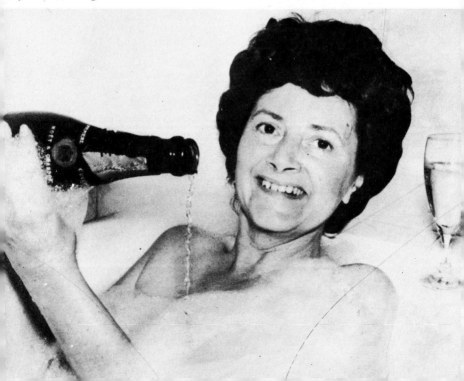

20. Christmas Day at Ambleside Avenue: (*from left to right*) Mitchell, Cynthia, Roger and a friend.

21. With Mitchell in his nuditorium shortly before his death.

8

'I crave an ample angel'

With diligence and application, Cynthia became an inventive and resourceful brothel-keeper. The demands of certain of her customers were a constant challenge to her skills as an entrepreneuse. A bank manager desirous of mud; a diplomat in need of the unorthodoxly fragrant armpit; a collector of taxes anxious to pretend that he is a lesbian; an engineer convinced that the departure of schoolgirls' elasticated knickers is indicative of the decline of Western civilization – these, and other, earnest obsessionists came to her establishment for the gratification of their appetites. Cynthia saw to it that they were never disappointed.

If she was ever surprised by a request, she did not give her astonishment either vocal or facial expression. It was imperative to behave as though the particular diversion required were the most commonplace thing anyone could possibly ask for. Of course she knew of the perfect surrogate nun; of course she could tie the gentleman up and leave him in a cupboard overnight; nothing could be easier than supplying a dominant lady with a foul tongue – the client's wish was her command.

Janet gave Cynthia much useful advice on how best to accommodate the 'kinky bondage fellows'. It is hard to imagine the quietly spoken, sad-eyed Janet as the strictest of disciplinarians, but that indeed is the role she sustained for fifteen wearying years. 'I broke down in the end,' she told me. 'I couldn't bear the strain and the pretence any longer.' Janet decided at the outset of her career that she would work with her mind rather than her body. In other words, she would not be the conventional prostitute, offering herself for conventional sex. She would cater for men who seldom wanted physical contact of the customary kind. She would satisfy the needs of those who wanted debasement and humiliation; needs that could as well be satisfied in the kitchen as the bedroom. 'I had to do a lot of acting. Sometimes I was playing as many as six different parts in a single day.'

Janet rented an apartment in Paddington, which had previously been occupied by an Austrian prostitute of a naturally severe disposition. 'Helga had had enough. The time had come for her to return to Austria and try to live a normal life with the money she'd made.' Janet bought Helga's equipment – ropes, whips, boots, stocks – and inherited the majority of her punters. Janet soon discovered that the men who visited her were from the upper reaches of English society. They wore expensive suits and carried rolled umbrellas. To judge by the performance that many of them demanded of Janet, they had each been reared by a forbidding nanny, of whom they had never ceased to be in awe.

One such was a portly, rubicund politician, who would turn up at the flat in Paddington with a script in hand. While Janet studied her lines, he disappeared into the bathroom, from which he emerged some minutes later in the not very convincing guise of a schoolboy. 'I really had to stop myself from laughing, the first time I saw him,' Janet said. 'I mean, he was very fat. He'd had a special outfit made for him – short trousers, a blazer, woollen socks and a school cap. His legs looked ridiculous, because they were a mass of varicose veins.'

The errant Simon is called into the presence of Nanny Wilkins.

NANNY: Who has been a naughty boy today?
SIMON: I have, Nanny.

NANNY: What does Nanny do to little boys when they are naughty?

SIMON: She smacks them, Nanny.

NANNY: And where does Nanny smack them, Simon?

SIMON: On their … On their …

NANNY: Speak up. Nanny can't hear naughty little boys who mumble.

SIMON: On their bot-bots, Nanny.

NANNY: Nanny thinks that Simon is too old for that nursery talk, Nanny does. Now where exactly on Simon's person is Nanny going to administer a smack?

SIMON: On his bottom, Nanny.

NANNY: Precisely.

(SIMON presents his bottom to NANNY, who smacks it hard.)

NANNY: Now stand up straight.

SIMON: Yes, Nanny. At once, Nanny. Thank you, Nanny.

(NANNY notices something that enrages her.)

NANNY: Who has not washed behind his ears this morning?

SIMON: I …

NANNY: Speak up!

SIMON: I must have forgotten to, Nanny. I won't forget again, I promise, Nanny.

NANNY: Nanny has heard too many of Simon's promises, Nanny has.

(NANNY clips the errant SIMON on both ears.)

And there the playlet would end. 'I never once saw his cock, in all the years I acted Nanny for him. He used to come inside his shorts when I clipped his ears. Then he'd go off to the bathroom. The next thing, he'd be in his pin stripes, looking like a proper politician. I often thought to myself, "If only the public knew what I know about you", when he paid me for his pleasure.'

Janet realized that she was on the verge of a breakdown when she found herself envying the prostitute who worked in a flat on the opposite side of the street. 'If a taxi drew up, and a bloke in casual clothes got out, I knew he was one of hers. If he was wearing a bowler and pin stripes, he was one of mine. I got to thinking how lucky she was, dealing with normal men instead of the upper-class loonies I had to put on a show for.'

Janet fell in love with just such a normal man, with whom she now lives. She is fortunate, she maintains, because an ex-prostitute is not everyone's idea of a good 'catch', and her lover is completely aware of the kind of woman he has 'caught'. 'He's very special. He knows I was on the game, yet he shows me nothing but respect.'

When Cynthia opened her doors, then, to the 'kinky bondage fellows' and their ilk, it was to Janet that she turned for assistance and information. Janet had long ago mastered the art of appearing forceful while she wielded the whip or thong, whereas in reality she was barely calling on her resources as a disciplinarian. There was no need to be cruel to yourself in order to be cruel to them. Economy was of the essence: one skilfully applied thwack was more pleasing to the recipient, and less physically demanding of the applicant, than a dozen haphazard strokes. The conservation of energy was of paramount importance, Janet insisted. It was the client who had to be exhausted.

Cynthia was afforded additional advice in regard to the business of domination by Gregory, whose own compulsion to be humbled had led him to Janet. Cynthia's future maid-servant described his ideal mistress in a letter to the woman who was to personify that ideal:

Dear Cindy,

I've had a bit of time to research more into the subject that intrigues you – namely, domination. The newspaper article I enclose deals with the aggression angle from a purely medical standpoint and I've made a few notes which used or read in conjunction with my 'slave manual' (which I hope you kept) might enlighten you still further. It's really the bits Adler leaves out.

For a start: You asked me once if I considered a rather attractive low-cut black dress you were wearing was the costume for the 'dominant mistress' role of erotic fame. I said 'No', thus cruelly shattering your belief, which was very uncharitable of me, because I didn't then give you *my* ideal vision of such a character. I now make amends for my curtness, and hope it will prove interesting reading.

My ideal 'Lady Domina' is an assemblage of all the fictional main female characters and bizarre wear figured in most sado-masochistic literature, and is as follows:

DRESS: Black Fleshlings faintly shiny (Cat suit). From neck to toes and worn over a very prominent bust line bra.

HELMET OR HOOD: In either Black Leather, Rubber Latex or Plastic Patent. Close fitting, with oval open facepiece. Worn with long hair (Blonde wig) flowing below.

MASK: In Black Satin with slanted eye slots and sequins, featured at brows too.

BOOTS: Near knee length fashion boots in glossy Black Leather or Shiny Plastic surface. Lace-up fronts and medium high spike heels. Worn with tiny rowel spurs for show.

BELT: 4″ wide waist belt in Black Leather, Patent or Plastic, or an outside-worn Corset Waist Nipper in Black ditto, but having vivid red laces. Pulled in very tight to accentuate the figure.

WIG: As most dominants are blonde, a platinum wig or hair piece worn to show below the helmet, as stated.

GLOVES: (Usually tucked into waist belt) Black leather with short cuffs, i.e. Riding Gloves.

COLLAR: Heavy (mock) Gold Chain, looped around neck, or Rhinestone 3 strand collar, or Poodle Collar set with Rhinestone Brilliants.

BRACELET: In Rhinestones and worn on right wrist (whip hand!) above glove surface (If 'Gold' Collar is used, use 'Gold' bracelet, of course.)

EARRINGS:	Worn if the helmet doesn't cover the ear lobes. Black Jet or Gold 'Dangle'-type. Heavy and noticeable.
RIDING SWITCH:	Black with silver metal fittings. Carried by loop from handle slung over wrist.
MAKE-UP:	Very pale with a suggestion of rouge on cheekbones. Vivid crimson lipstick. Cold blue or green eye-shadow. Pointed finger nails. NOTE Lips drawn rather thin to give severity to the face, <u>not full!</u>

With this dress goes the pose. Madame's walk because of her high heels and drawn-in waist is definitely aggressive. Quite naturally by it she commands attention, this combined with her mannerisms.

Her manner is haughty, her voice imperious and cold, even mockingly vicious. She doesn't question but demands, doesn't request but issues an order: a decree, in fact. Visiting Madam is more like obtaining an audience with a queen of ancient times. A goddess of cruelty.

For instance: A 'slave' though still in his street clothes and he meeting her for the first time – where it would be normal to shake hands in greeting, Madam would require him to kneel at her feet and kiss his mistress' shoe tip reverently. This act Madam would not regard as dramatic or theatrical, but as merely showing good manners and common courtesy!!

Her most favoured position for greeting a slave might be sitting in a large armchair, her legs elegantly crossed and she smoking a cigarette through a long holder, perhaps while she leafed idly through a glossy fashion magazine. Can you get the picture?

The slave would enter (she wouldn't look up), face his Mistress, approach to within 6 ft of her chair, then get down on his knees and crawl very slowly towards her feet, head bent low to the floor.

In due course, Madam's recognition of his presence might be a soft snapping of her fingers, followed by a vague wave towards her feet. Her slave would then respond by respectfully kissing the sole of her boot, the one nearest him. To perform this task, the slave would be most careful <u>not</u> to let his fingers come anywhere near his Mistress's boots. The punishment for such a crime would be, say, 12 cuts of the whip across each palm, since his fingers, however carefully they had been scrubbed and manicured, would be considered by Madam to be 'unclean'!

The most favourable response his Mistress might show the slave would be to raise the other sole to the slave's lips to be kissed likewise. This would be a singular show of tolerance. But of course Madam may not choose to acknowledge her slave at that time and decide to let him wait, kneeling patiently at her feet while she finishes reading.

Madam may even choose to use the slave's back as a foot-rest, her pointed boots tearing and bruising the tender skin of his back, and she indifferent to his groans! And if wearing dress spurs – Oh, what pain!

This then is the sort of 'Domina' most masochistically inclined men want, though some don't know it at the time, it seems.

Believe me, Cindy, treat them this way initially – dressed as described and you'll have any one of them 'on toast', struck dumb at the treatment!

Later on, you can break said slave's spirit entirely, by being utterly contemptuous of his 'rights' and laughing at any suggestion of sexual gratification coming from him.

Just remember that a *real* slave would readily consume dog food at his Mistress's order, let alone obey her every wish. Remember this the next time you have a man under the lash!

Keep this for reference when/if we get together the costume.

The costume was eventually got together. Dressed in her cat suit, Cynthia became Lady Domina, Gregory's dark angel. Many were the joyous evenings in Cranmore when Lady Domina – or Madam Baloney, as Mitch preferred to call her – ruled over her underlings. It must be stressed, though, that the Cranmorian style of domination and cruelty is of a relatively mild kind. Compared to those ladies who advertise their wicked appeal in the magazine *Madames in a World of Fantasy*, the dark angel of Streatham is of a truly angelic disposition.

This curious journal, one of several produced by the felicitously named Swish Publishing Company, contains articles on every aspect of male subordination. The self-proclaimed bitch, Miss Candida, offers advice on penile (sic) restraint, squatting power, high heel worship and other strange customs, not all of them hygienic. There are letters from inspired and aspiring 'doms' and photographs and drawings of enslaved men and their stern or mocking captors. There is a Madame of the Month, who for some reason known only to the editorial staff is usually obese. These neckless neo-Nazis – for such most of them pretend to be – are probably loving and responsible mothers, favourite aunties, cherished grannies. To their victims, however, they are superior beings with the power, and indeed the right, to terrify.

For the disinterested reader, the fascination of *Madames in a World of Fantasy* lies in the lethally battered English its zestful contributors employ to describe their exotic practices. The commanding Miss Candida and her saucy sisters in knicker tyranny lash the tongue of Shakespeare and Milton as if it were the collective bottom of innumerable degraded men. They render it a lifeless thing – a mess of dismembered syntax, of stupefied punctuation.

These annihilators of language and restrainers of penes often go about their work in the appropriate setting of a dungeon or a torture chamber. Neither sinister cell could be found in Cranmore, where the 'kinky bondage fellows' of yesteryear were also required to be 'licensed jesters'. Lady Domina liked to exert discipline in a happy atmosphere, with only the occasional glare from the leather-clad Magda to menace the grovelling pranksters. Sometimes when Cynthia was thwacking Mitch's backside ('Call yourself a squadron leader? You couldn't fly a bloody kite!'), she had to curb her natural desire to laugh. Candida and her cohorts would be shocked by such irreverence. A superior Mistress may mock, but she must not acknowledge the absurdity of her undertaking.

Cynthia has a healthy sense of the ridiculous. Not for her the rack; not for her the thumb-screw – those deadly instruments, so suggestive of real terror, of real agony, have never been seen among the Cranmorian properties. Fun can be had with a riding whip, but pain of a different order is attendant upon the appurtenances of medieval castles. Gentlemen who wanted to be frightened senseless by a 'dom fem' were advised by Cynthia to contact certain ladies in the Earls Court area, one of whom has a fully equipped operating theatre, in which she performs as a particularly splashy surgeon. The 'kinky bondage fellows' who visited Edencourt Road and Ambleside Avenue were merely reduced to a state of pleasant exhaustion, and were fortified by poached eggs on toast before returning to the normal world outside. There were sore behinds in Streatham then. No one ever left Cranmore with an unsightly scar, a debilitating wound.

The discipline afforded Slave Rodney and Slave Philip, therefore, was, and is, of a subtle nature. Both men still wait upon Lady Domina, but they are not severely punished in the process. They are insulted, but not injured. They are blissfully happy when they are told off for not doing their household chores properly. If Madam is more than usually displeased with Slave Philip's work, she ties the unfortunate skiver to a leg of the kitchen table and commands him to eat out of the dog's bowl.

Except, of course, that Slave Philip does not consider himself unfortunate. To be chained up and made to take his food on all fours is very ecstasy to him. Slave Rodney likes to be lowly, too, though in a different manner. This gentle, charming man in his sixties began his working life in service at the age of twelve. He cleaned the boots and shoes of the gentry in a large country house, and it is this task that even today affords him most delight. He remembers an occasion during his puberty when the cook and an extremely pretty maidservant both ordered him to polish their lace-up boots while they were wearing them. The maid taunted him as he worked, and his penis became erect, to his acute embarrassment. He then ejaculated for the first time.

Years ago, when Rodney was nobody's slave, he asked his young wife if he could kneel at her feet and clean her shoes. She asked him, in turn, to explain his odd request. He did so, in what – for her – was upsetting detail. She told him that she found him disgusting and perverted and that she would never, never satisfy him in such a revolting way. Their sexual life stopped at that moment. The marriage was sustained for the sake of their daughter, who herself is a mother now. Rodney is a responsible man, who loves his child and revels in the company of his grandchildren.

Rodney would have continued living in extreme physical frustration had he not chanced upon a contact magazine containing an advertisement from Cynthia. The shy and reticent works manager summoned up the courage to write a reply, and as a consequence visited her in Edencourt Road. She listened to his story, and expressed neither disgust nor revulsion. She understood his need to repeat, however approximately, that unforgotten event of his boyhood. She told him she would help him do so. His was a familiar predicament, she assured him.

Cynthia was immediately impressed by Rodney's exquisite manners. I was, too. I watched him at a special party that he and Cynthia attended in the summer of 1981 for a number of disabled people, and was moved by the unforced kindness he displayed to them. There were two men present who could not go to the lavatory without assistance, and that assistance was amiably and enthusiastically supplied by the unembarrassed Rodney.

Slave Rodney has been a happier man since he made Cynthia's acquaintance. He spends most weekends trying to come to terms with the garden behind Cranmore, which is large enough to require more than a day's attention each week in the spring, summer and autumn months. He trims the lawn and cuts back the rose bushes and dead-heads the flowers to the best of his ability. Considering the short amount of time he manages to devote to it, the garden is in a remarkably healthy condition.

His reward for working with such application is to be called into Madam's presence and ordered to clean her footwear. Madam taunts the servile wretch, just as the pretty maid-servant taunted him nearly half a century earlier.

Slave Philip, a polite young man who sells insurance in the Home Counties, wrote Cynthia a letter of application that she found irresistible. A sizable quantity of the letters she received while she was running the brothel were, in fact, left unanswered. Men who boasted of their 'massive equipment' or promised endless orgasmic bliss were written off as Jack-my-lads. 'They come when they're writing that stuff,' she told me. 'They're a waste of bloody time.' Slave Philip's style struck her at once as being genuine:

Dear Madam,

i have just received my copy of Pathway magazine and i was very interested to read Your advertisement (M.12) for a handyman/gardener/domestic servant so i am immediately writing to beg You to consider my application for this position. i expect You have received many hundreds of replies from subservient males like myself all begging to serve You and i fear that i am too late and that You are already suited. However, i am nevertheless writing in the forlorn hope that i may be fortunate enough to be granted an interview.

i am truly submissive by nature with many years training in all aspects of slavery. i do assure You that i am honest, hardworking and reliable and i would dearly love to work for You, obeying all Your instructions implicitly and to the letter, no matter how unreasonable or unfair they may be. i am very broadminded and completely unshockable and i am prepared to accept any humiliation, degradation, abuse and punishment in the course of my duties if it so pleases You.

i am skilled and experienced at all aspects of decorating and home maintenance and i possess a complete range of tools to cover all eventualities. i am also a keen and enthusiastic gardener and i am capable of being left to work unsupervised. i can tackle all domestic duties although my ironing leaves a little to be desired. i always work painstakingly and i strive for perfection as past experience has taught me that few Mistresses are satisfied with anything less.

Of course i am perfectly happy to work entirely unpaid and i will also provide all the materials, etc. required at my own expense. i also expect to pay a reasonable fee for the honour and privilege of serving You.

You state in your ad that foot fetishists are welcome. Well, at the end of a hard day's work i would love nothing more than to curl up at Your feet and kiss and lick Your shoes or boots, devotedly and passionately for as long as You permit. i desperately hope that You will be kind enough to consider my plea and i enclose a stamped addressed envelope and anxiously wait to hear from You.

Yours obediently,
slave philip.

The obedient Philip was granted an interview, as a result of which he was instantly employed. He proved to be 'bloody wonderful' at scrubbing and polishing. But Philip is no ordinary domestic help. When he is scouring the kitchen sink or cleaning the silver or giving the walls of the lounge a fresh lick of paint, he is naked except for his wrist watch and wedding ring. His being in the nude makes it easier for his fault-finding Mistress to flay his behind if she finds him negligent of his duties.

He has never been that, but it is essential for him to be told that he has been. A bawling-out excites him and spurs him on to greater effort. Early in his marriage, he went out drinking with his wife and some friends one night and got rather drunk, which is something he rarely does. Returning home, he and his wife had a row. She complained about the state of the kitchen floor. For once, she said, he could clean it; she'd done it too often. He had already started to undress when the order came. He removed his remaining clothes and set to work with a mop. He was strangely elated, he recalls. His docile wife had seldom been angry with him before, and her sudden, unexpected display of temper made him realize precisely what stimulated him sexually.

She has not been angry with him since. Like many of the men who used to visit Cranmore and the house in Edencourt Road, Philip is unhappy with the physical side of his marriage. He would be a contented man if his wife could will herself to abuse him occasionally and insist that he do the housework. But she cannot, and has made it clear to him that his is an impossible need for her to gratify.

There are times, Philip confesses, when he is anxious, nothing less, for some sterner discipline than Cynthia is willing to provide. It is then that he drives to Matlock in Derbyshire, where his other Superior Mistress lives. This fearsome lady has a daughter who shares her compulsion to reduce men to their proper level, and the two of them often join together to reduce Philip to his. The Matlock Mistress takes Philip by car to a secluded spot in the High Peak, where she commands him to undress. Assisted by her eager daughter, she binds Philip firmly to a tree with a length or so of strong rope. She picks up his clothes and throws them on the back seat of her Renault and informs the naked slave that she will return if she feels like it, but if she doesn't feel like it, she won't. The two women then depart for a day's shopping in Derby.

Imagine Philip's distress as the afternoon wears on. Imagine him at nightfall, with only birds and scampering animals for company. Imagine him in midsummer, when that rugged region of the English countryside is a favourite haunt of tourists – what if one or more wandered into the thicket and discovered him? Imagine him in the small hours, chilled to the bone and convinced that his Mistress has finally forsaken him.

Philip ejaculates more than once before his baleful Mistress's arrival. Unlike poor Onan, the dispersive inventor of coitus interruptus, he is not slain by a displeased God, though he is the recipient of several jibes from both the Matlock Mistress and the Mistress *manquée*. They ridicule him as they release him, and he is properly humbled.

It is a refreshed Philip who journeys back to the Home Counties and the selling of insurance. He has faced the worst that a slave can endure and is now in the right frame of mind to enjoy the reproaches of his Streatham Mistress. He cannot wait to give Cranmore a thorough spring cleaning.

In her party-giving days, Cynthia would command Philip to make the house ready for her guests. On those occasions, the girls were invited to tease him as he went about his various tasks. They interrupted him as he slaved away: 'Another cup of coffee, Slave Philip, and be quick about it!'; 'Slave Philip, you have been ordered to bath me!'; 'Do up my zip, Slave Philip, or you'll get the back of my hand!' Slave Philip responded to their demands by thanking them for giving him the honour of proving himself useful, though in his next breath he apologized for his inadequacy.

Dear Mistress Judith

i am firstly writing to thank You for a marvellous party. i really did enjoy myself, although You kept me busy and i worked very hard. It was a wonderful feeling having so many lovely girls around me and coming up to me asking for drinks, etc. i hope my work was satisfactory and that i didn't let You down. It was very exciting to meet Miss Agatha. Miss Agatha seems to be a most imperious lady, one whom i would instantly obey and respect. i hope she will forgive me for not being able to put ice in her cold drink. i do apologize for running out at that time although some more was beginning to harden in the refrigerator.

i hope You don't mind, but i am using up a day of my holiday to visit my Mistress in Matlock this week so i will be unable to get over, but i will contact You the week after to make some more arrangements to serve You soon.

Although Your sexy party was very exciting, i still think that a kinky party would be even more fun, especially if it was like the one You organized for the bank manager. i do hope You will be able to show me the photographs of him covered in messy things. Would it be possible for me to suffer this degradation on a smaller scale? Perhaps on a plastic sheet in a room upstairs? i would only want one or two people present to mess me up.

Yours obediently,
slave philip.

Keeping in mind the type of slavery on offer in the hills of Derbyshire, it seems odd that Philip should ask for small-scale degradation. Not that the bank manager's messing-up could really be accounted large scale: when one considers the grisly condition in which some humiliated customers leave their humiliators, his was a miniature befoulment. The photograph Cynthia took of him when he was covered from head to foot with the contents of the Hoover bag made me think of the Tollund Man, who was preserved in a peat bog in Denmark for 2,000 years until he was brought out of the umber-brown earth in 1950. What can be discerned of the bank manager's features bears an eerie resemblance to the face of the hanged man from the Iron Age.

It says something for the trust that Cynthia inspired in her clients that the bank manager allowed her to photograph him. A less honourable madam would have contemplated black-mail, or at least secured a substantial loan at a reasonable rate of interest. Cynthia pursued neither unscrupulous course. It is indicative of her attitude to her business that in all the years she ran a brothel she never had any dealings with the crim-inal fringe. 'I kept a clean house. None of my girls was on drugs, and I always vetted the men before accepting them as customers.'

One of her former partygoers, a retired chief superintendent in the Metropolitan Police, told me that if all the brothels in the British Isles were run on the same lines as Cynthia's, he and his fellow officers would welcome a change in the law.

'But they're not, unfortunately,' Cuthbert said. 'As far as I am concerned, Cynthia is, or rather was, unique. The majority of brothels do much more than cater for the sexual appetites of their clients. They're often cover-ups for drug-pushing, among other things. I know of brothel-keepers who are also receivers of stolen goods. It's no secret that there are houses, particularly in the West End of London, that are in business specifically for tourists – wealthy Arabs and the like. The men who visit them are charged way over the odds. Cynthia's set-up was innocent by comparison.'

Cuthbert befriended Cynthia after arresting her on a charge of brothel-keeping. She was working in her last West

End flat at the time. The arrest itself was a riotously funny event. At the station, Cynthia insisted on giving each and every officer her diagnosis of his sexual problems or requirements. 'You come too quickly, that's your trouble,' she informed a surprised constable. The men were both amused and impressed by her brazen behaviour, particularly Cuthbert, who in all his long career could not remember an occasion quite like it. 'She had us all in hysterics. She pleaded guilty straight away, but said that she didn't feel in the least guilty about her work. "I provide a useful service," she kept on saying. Which was exactly what she did. The atmosphere at her parties was never dirty or sordid – it was just a group of pleasant people having a lot of fun.'

Cuthbert tried to warn her for years that she was courting trouble with the police, which could end in possible imprisonment. 'She's a wonderful human being, warm and kind and generous. But she can be headstrong. If she wants to ignore something, she will. She ignored my advice a thousand times. Even when she went to prison, though, she behaved as if it wasn't the end of the world. She's a real stoic in that respect. She accepts whatever life dishes out to her and simply carries on.'

Cynthia had a deeper involvement, though certainly not such a lasting one, with another policeman, with whom she fell in love. The liaison was doomed, she realized, because of the shame Walter suffered at betraying his wife. When he made extra-brothel dates with Cynthia, he would consume a great deal of alcohol prior to meeting her. 'I was head over heels about him. I fancied him like mad. We had a few bloody wonderful nights together, but more often than not they were spoilt because he had brewer's droop.'

Cynthia formed a more passionate attachment to a young Moroccan named Mohammed. She met him while she was on holiday in Tangier with Agatha, who made the vacation doubly memorable for Cynthia by her seven-minute performance with a tour guide at the airport, behind a conveniently placed bush. Apart from the two hectic participants, only Cynthia knew why the leaves were fluttering on that windless day.

Mohammed was by far the most accomplished and considerate of her lovers in the purely physical sense. He took pains to satisfy her, and he did so. He had that legendary staying power that many of her correspondents boasted of possessing. He was not happy to complete their love-making until she achieved orgasm. Sex with him was a revelation to her. 'I thought I knew all there was to bloody know when it came to how's-your-father, but Mohammed taught me a few things and no mistake. He could make it last till you started to go out of your mind. He wasn't like Sam, who needed it six times a night. He did it once, to perfection.'

Cynthia became besotted with Mohammed, to such an extent that Mitchell and Gregory grew alarmed. She was in the grip of total infatuation. They had long been aware that, for all her seeming worldliness, she was a romantic at heart. They feared that she would lose her sense of reality and destroy everything she had carefully built up over several years. Her contact with the real world was stronger than they supposed. On each visit to Morocco, she found herself a little bit more disillusioned with her handsome and still skilful lover. He had taken to drink, like most of the men with whom she had been involved. She was happy to spend money on him, but aggrieved to see so young a man ruining himself with an enormous intake of whisky.

On her very last trip to Tangier, she discovered something about Mohammed that she had half suspected but never properly acknowledged. She saw him one afternoon talking to a famous English actor by the hotel's swimming pool, and wondered how someone like Mohammed could be on such obviously familiar terms with an internationally known film star. Later that day, she asked her boy friend how he had made the actor's acquaintance. He replied, unblushingly, that they had met in the way of business – bedroom business. It did not surprise her to learn that Mohammed was – and, presumably, still is – a prostitute.

She was not distressed by his confession. Quite the contrary: she assumed that it was his bisexuality that made him so adept and inventive a lover. What did upset her, what finally caused her to sever the relationship, was Mohammed's unstoppable addiction to alcohol. Like many drunks, he would change character completely at a certain stage in his drinking – he would suddenly become inexplicably morose, or self-pitying, or even violent. Cynthia finds it hard to tolerate drunkenness, although she is sympathetic to the people afflicted by the disease. Mohammed's inability to remain sober forced her out of her besottedness.

In spite of her unfortunate experience in matters of the heart, Cynthia is unswervingly loyal to the curious notion that the male is the superior of the species. That is not to say that she does not sustain affectionate friendships with women, many of whom once worked for her, because the reverse is true. Neither does she believe that men are inherently stable and sensible, since she has amassed far too much evidence to the contrary: 'A man who isn't despunking regularly is sure to make a bloody fool of himself.' No – it is solely in the business sphere that the regularly despunked male demonstrates his superiority and his trustworthiness: 'Women are either hard or scatterbrained.' When I asserted that my solicitor, my accountant and my agent – all women – were neither, she declared: 'Well, I suppose there must be a few exceptions.'

Even so, the two men with whom Cynthia has had fruitful and progressive relationships could not be described as upholders of conventional masculine ideals. Mitchell was – and Gregory is – a transvestite. The late Squadron Leader Smith discovered the delights of cross-dressing in his old age, a discovery Gregory made in his youth, but then suppressed for many years. Cynthia allowed Mitchell, as she still allows Gregory, the freedom of Cranmore for the expression of his other persona. Photographs reveal that his stockinged legs were the equal of Betty Grable's. These he was always delighted to display, unlike his face, which he considered 'bloody horrible' – when in drag, it was usually hidden behind a veil or a yashmak. His refusal to wear false teeth did nothing to make his features more beguiling.

Robert Mitchell Smith was born in 1906 in the Highbury area of London. His father ran a number of small businesses.

but because of his drinking habits was frequently in debt. Mitchell, who had a brother and two sisters, was not very bright academically, but he still managed to win a scholarship to Westminster City School while attending a 'really rough school' not far from his birthplace. He was 'asked to leave' the relatively posh academy, however, and was more fortunate than most working-class children of his time in being given immediate employment.

His first job was in the garage his father ran near Clapham Common. This was followed by a stint in another family concern, in a furniture warehouse in Battersea. Like the garage, the warehouse was eventually sold off, and Mitchell found himself involved in yet another of his father's ventures – an illegal betting operation. It was with the money that he made from the unlucky bets of the punters that he voyaged to Canada, where he studied agriculture at McGill University in Montreal.

'I realized at an early age,' Mitchell said, 'that in England – which was a terribly snobbish country then, and to my mind still is – you had to have a so-called education. It didn't, and doesn't, matter if you'd learned sod all, so long as you could say you'd studied at such-and-such a place. I always told people when I was much older that I'd been to Westminster School – I dropped the "City" bit, you see, and the bloody snobs were really impressed. Westminster! And McGill in those days was the biggest university in Canada. Westminster *and* McGill! My, my – old Smith wasn't just anybody, was he? He'd had a *proper* education!'

Mitchell was awarded a diploma from the agricultural college at McGill and went to work on a farm to gain practical experience. He was a farm labourer for two years. He was twenty-one when he decided to try his luck in the United States. For him, America seemed an El Dorado – the country that contained a magical place called Hollywood. He boarded a bus at Vancouver and booked a ticket to Seattle.

'This was the time of prohibition and every frontier was guarded. I had no visa and no passport. I was determined to get in, though I didn't know how. I thought I'd get chucked off the coach at Seattle, but luck was with me because all the guards were rolling drunk on bootleg liquor. I think they must have had some sort of deal with the drivers. Anyway, I remember this particular guard, he swayed across to the bus, which was absolutely packed, and he said, "All right, Bill. Oh, yes – you're O.K." He just waved his hand, and on we went. I was on American soil, by sheer chance, by sheer accident.'

Mitchell wandered down the west coast and ended up in Hollywood. He found it difficult getting even the most ordinary job – he was an illegal immigrant, and therefore frightened of being handed over to the authorities. He worked as a farm hand. Farmers welcomed cheap labour and didn't ask embarrassing questions.

He returned to England, confident in the knowledge that he had beaten the English system. He had studied at Westminster and McGill, and he had travelled extensively. He was a somebody now.

Encouraged by a devoted aunt, he enrolled to train as a pilot in the Royal Air Force, which was, of course, still in its infancy. He was accepted, and sent to Grantham in Lincolnshire. 'It was one hell of a hole. We all escaped at weekends.'

He and his fellow trainee pilots escaped to Nottingham, which was the nearest city of any size. Mitchell was by this time an accomplished ballroom dancer. 'Going ballroom dancing was a good way of getting to meet girls. I chased around the dance halls while I was in London – Hammersmith Palais, Wimbledon Palais. You had to be able to dance properly if you wanted to be in the swim. The girls didn't want to know if you were a clodhopper.'

Mitchell met his future wife at the Nottingham Palais de Danse.

'Violet was very pretty. She was only seventeen and a half, but she let me make love to her the first night we met. I was staggered. She wasn't a virgin, which was unusual for those days – I'm talking about the early 1930s. I didn't have to do any work at all; it was plain sailing from the start. But what really knocked me sideways was when she said, "Don't come inside me." Think of it: an innocent-looking girl saying that! Christ, I was staggered.'

Violet was far more experienced sexually than her staggered suitor. At the age of sixteen, Mitchell had visited a hotel in the centre of London, the foyer of which contained a lounge where prostitutes plied their trade. He was sitting in the lounge, lingering over afternoon tea, when a middle-aged man joined him at his table and broke into conversation with him. The man bought Mitchell a drink and afterwards invited him to dinner. The boy, who was there for the express purpose of buying the favours of a whore, quickly scanned the lounge for a likely lady before accepting the invitation. There was none present, so Mitchell left with the charming Greek.

After the meal, his host suggested to the boy that the two of them should go to his, the Greek's, lodgings in Bloomsbury. Mitchell had no idea that his new-found friend was homosexual. 'Nobody told you anything about normal sex then, let alone homosexuality. I was a complete innocent. I was as randy as hell, but I didn't have a clue what to do about it. That's why I went to the hotel. I thought a prostitute would educate me.'

He was indeed educated that night, but in a different manner from the one he had anticipated. 'The Greek gave me some pyjamas to wear. He even went out of the room while I got undressed and put them on. We went to bed in the dark, I remember, and we said goodnight. I turned over to sleep and the next thing was I felt his hard prick against my arse. I was terribly excited, for all that I was surprised. It's not so bloody horrible, whatever people say. I was so desperate, I didn't stop to worry if I was doing something perverted. He was a thoughtful bloke, that Greek: he brought me off when he'd finished, which was exactly what I wanted. I wasn't the least bit ashamed in the morning – in fact, I was grateful. I went home in a cheerful mood because I'd had my oats. I never saw the man again, and I never had another go at homosexuality until I was in my seventies, and that was in Greece.'

Mitchell was frustrated for most of his time in Canada and America. With a bunch of boys from the college, who were all 'as green as hell', he went to the 'arse end' of Montreal in search of loose women. They roamed the streets for a while, and then entered a movie house, to kill a couple of hours before things hotted up outside. An ice-cream seller gave them the address of a brothel. It was miles away, in an even rougher area of the city. 'There was a bloody queue winding all along the street and round the corner. We would have had to wait for hours.' The group repaired instead to a café where a couple of girls obliged with the quickest of quickies in a room upstairs. The pair accommodated the dozen or so students from McGill in what Mitchell remembered as a little over half-an-hour.

He was more successful during the few months he spent in London before going off to Grantham for his training. He had a motor car, which made a greater impression on some girls than good looks and winning ways. His skill as a dancer helped him, too. He made a number of conquests, but only after a great deal of preliminary chat and the consumption of several cocktails.

Violet needed no such preliminaries. Her eagerness for sex startled Mitchell, who was accustomed to coyness, decorousness, horrified or pretended protestation. Violet was absolutely straightforward and refreshingly honest: 'She couldn't get enough of it, and she said so. She opened my eyes. I didn't so much as look at another woman while Violet was around.'

Violet was around for the entirety of her husband's distinguished career in the Royal Air Force. He took her with him wherever he was stationed. Because of his skill as a pilot and his ability to communicate his enthusiasm for flying, Mitchell was elected to train young men for the difficult task of night-time combat. He was tested to the utmost of his ability, and was eventually put in charge of his own squadron. At the end of the war, though, he felt that he had had enough excitement, enough danger. He and Violet looked after a pub for a while, and then bought a small newsagency and tobacconist's business in Skegness. It was there that Violet died, in her mid-forties.

Mitchell was heartbroken. He lived in a state of limbo for years afterwards. He knew that Violet was irreplaceable, and when his sexual urge was no longer dormant – as it was for a considerable time following her death – he suffered appalling guilt at the idea of being aroused by anyone other than Violet.

He missed her terribly. At her insistence, there were no children by the marriage, so Mitchell was alone with his grief.

He was alone for what seemed to him an age. He bought a large house in Purley, Surrey, which he had converted into three flats. He took the ground floor one for himself and sold the other two. His vast garden was also on three levels. The tenants were allowed access to the lower and middle levels, but the highest was out of bounds. This was Mitchell's nuditorium in the last years of his life. He would sleep in a tiny shed during the summer months in order to be closer to nature. He would potter about all day in the nude in his cut-off domain, where he would welcome a few selected visitors. These included, besides Cynthia, his particular favourites among the girls – Janet, Magda and Agatha.

There was a pole in the garden, to which Mitchell liked to be tied. The naked women would dance round it, uttering strange whooping noises and sometimes chanting in unison. 'We felt such bloody fools,' said Cynthia. 'He called us his squaws.' These tribal rites were performed in the unlikely setting of the stockbroker belt. It gave the former Squadron Leader much amusement to contemplate the possible reactions of his neighbours to the news that primitive customs were taking place only yards away from their neatly trimmed hedges, their regularly mown lawns. The news never reached them, though they must have been occasionally curious about the odd shriek that disturbed the Surrey tranquillity. Agatha was especially proficient when a blood-curdling yell was required.

Before Mitchell answered Cynthia's advertisement in a contact magazine, he was a frequent visitor to massage parlours. He also visited a 'terrifying cow' in Earls Court, who had a large wheel in her apartment. No fewer than six men could be tied to this contraption, which was turned slowly. Since Mitchell was not prepared to pay more than a few pounds to the forbidding Hortense, he was granted the honour of clearing up the mess that resulted from the circulative torture. This duty, he soon discovered, afforded him no delight whatsoever.

It was in Madam Baloney's company that he finally found

contentment. Throwing rubbish at the bank manager fitted in with his view of the essential absurdity of life: he was a skilful marksman. Had Violet gone on living, he would never have developed into a 'kinky bondage fellow', and certainly not a transvestite. Alone at night in his flat in Purley, he would often put on a flowing evening gown or a skirt, twin set and pearls, depending on his mood. 'In a funny way, it was like having a woman about the place again. I enjoyed dressing up as a kind of substitute.'

Sometimes, at Cranmore, he rigged himself out as the butler. With Gregory as 'Anthea', the most conscientious of maidservants, Mitchell would wait on his demanding Madam Baloney. They were occasionally joined at these 'kinky' parties by Randolph, a political commentator who assumed the role of 'Tillie', a rowdy tweeny who was forever causing havoc below stairs. The butler, exasperated by 'her' unruly behaviour, would take the slattern across his knees and give 'Tillie' the spanking 'she' deserved. It was a contrite maid who staggered back to the kitchen.

There can be no doubt that Cynthia was largely responsible for the happiness Mitchell experienced in his old age. The houses in Edencourt Road and Ambleside Avenue were always open to him – indeed, he was given the keys to both. He would often have furious rows with his beloved Madam Baloney, but they were seldom of any importance. Both being headstrong, it was inevitable that they would get on each other's nerves.

Mitchell was a naturalist and a vegetarian. This man, who enjoyed a thorough whipping when the mood was on him, could not tolerate cruelty to animals. He would shout abuse at anyone who killed a fly or wasp. He always drank the water that vegetables had been cooked in – it was his 'elixir', he said. His garden was overgrown with weeds. 'They have a right to live as well.' If Mitchell had had his way, the garden at Cranmore would have been in a similar condition. The otherwise gentle Slave Rodney made it plain to the old man that he was the gardener there and would not tolerate such disorder.

Cynthia fondly recalls that Mitchell was once teased by a

boastful partygoer about the comparative smallness of his
penis. Mitchell was not annoyed or upset by the taunt. He
told the man to look closely at the sculpture of the ancient
world and to examine that of Michelangelo as well. 'You will
notice no difference between their cocks and mine,' he said.
'In fact, you'll see how much like David's mine is. I have a
classical cock, my good fellow.'

Mitchell died of a massive heart attack in July 1981. He
was alone in his flat in Purley. His corpse was discovered
some ten days later by Cynthia and Roger, who had grown
worried because they had not heard from him.

The Squadron Leader's funeral was appropriately uncommon. Guy de Maupassant would have relished it. The sky
was overcast and there were intermittent showers. The mourners who followed the hearse from Streatham to the cemetery
in Croydon included Janet and Magda, Gregory, and an
assortment of old Cranmorians. The political commentator
looked so sober and serious that it was hard to imagine him
as the slatternly 'Tillie'. Mitchell's erstwhile companions in
debauchery were all strictly disciplined in their behaviour.
At its outset, it was like any other funeral.

In the cemetery chapel, the disreputable mourners looked
across at the respectable ones from Purley and its environs.
A cursory service was held before the coffin was hurriedly
consigned to earth. The rain beat down on whippers and
whoopers and on those who will never whip or whoop, under
any circumstances.

Four of Purley's more adventurous residents accepted
Madam Baloney's invitation to the reception at Cranmore.
They were, as it transpired, rightly apprehensive.

The reception developed, quite naturally, into a party.
Happy memories of Mitchell's various eccentricities were
exchanged, giving rise to much laughter. As the old Cranmorians of both sexes grew friendlier, Cynthia decided that
the afternoon should take a different course. She suddenly
called for silence. Everyone present was then asked to toast
the dear departed. 'That's the respectable part of the funeral
over,' Cynthia announced. 'We've seen the old boy to his last
resting place, now let's remember him in the way he would

143

like to be remembered. The upstairs rooms are open. Let fucking commence!'

And commence it did, to the astonishment of one lady from Purley, who kept repeating, with increasing hysteria, 'I've never been in a house like this in my life!' Clerics, business-men and barristers mounted the staircase they knew so well, but for once they had no need of luncheon vouchers. Their joy was unconfined, which meant that it was free, by order of Madam Baloney. The sound of creaking bedsprings, she observed, would be more congenial to Mitchell's ears than any hymn or any prayer. The gasps of contented elderly men were his requiem mass.

Mitchell could not be described as a serious transvestite. He liked people to laugh with him when he lifted his bee-keeper's veil. It was only in private, perhaps, that he took the pretence of being a woman beyond caricature. In company, he was a slapstick female – a pantomime dame of a wilder disposition than the customary Widow Twankey.

Gregory, who would never dare to call Cynthia by the disrespectful name of Madam Baloney, is altogether more earnest. For him, dressing up means the attainment of an-other personality, one that he is happier with than his own. As 'Anthea', who besides being a maid is also a sophisticated middle-aged woman, he fulfils himself, as others fulfil them-selves by making love. Gregory's 'lineaments of gratified desire' are those of 'Anthea' as 'she' smiles at his reflection in the mirror.

'I look down at the clothes I'm wearing and I think, "Yes, you are a middle to upper-class matron, smartly turned out, getting on in years, probably with a son now married, already with children, so you're also probably a grandmother. The lines on your face give the game away, and the way you walk and the way you speak and the amount of ornamentation you use – you are wearing a very, very light eyeshadow, if indeed any at all, as befits a woman of fifty-five. You are definitely not mutton dressed up to look like lamb." I have to be cautious. A real woman can dress and make up to convince people that she's younger, though she's not always successful, but it isn't advisable for a transvestite to do the same. There's the danger of being discovered, or "read" as we say, and that can be a terrible humiliation.'

Gregory was conscious as a child that he didn't quite belong in his family. His father, who owned a small grocery business in Battersea, was a self-made man who had 'dragged himself up by his boot straps', as he was constantly reminding Gregory and the two younger children.

'I had a very bad relationship with him, unfortunately. I can think of him with a little more kindness now. I realize that he'd had to surmount obstacles in his early life that would have defeated someone with less guts than he had. His father died when Dad was just a boy, and his mother had to scrub floors to earn enough to bring him up. He took to stealing and might have become a full-time thief if it hadn't been for the First World War. He fought in two of the worst battles – Ypres and Passchendaele. He only ever said one thing about his military career. "Five thousand men in one night" – just that single remark.'

Gregory remembers his father as a rough-and-ready individual who drank heavily. He was too busy to find time to talk and listen to his sons and daughter, so the children confided in their mother instead. Gregory, who was born in 1926, spent his formative years in the company of women, since the majority of his male relatives went off to fight in the Second World War. He was never interested in the things that boys are supposed to be interested in, though he wasn't effeminate in any respect. At the age of seven, he was dressed up as a fairy – which he seems to recall that he enjoyed, despite the fact that his appearance must have been 'laughable'. Otherwise he was aware that when he grew up he, too, was expected to go off and serve his country. His maternal grandmother, to whom he was very attached, had lost three brothers in the South African War, and she instilled in him a sense of duty and the importance and nobility of sacrifice.

Gregory rose in the non-commissioned ranks in the army and was drafted to Palestine in the mid-1940s. He saw dreadful carnage there, and is still haunted by the experience. On his return to England, he settled down with his widowed mother, with whom he was to live for another twenty years. His brother and sister had both married. It was assumed within the family that Gregory would remain a bachelor.

He courted a couple of girls, but in a non-committal fashion. Then he became enamoured of a woman who had been on the verge of marrying his best friend. He had been asked to intercede on the friend's behalf. His efforts to patch up the relationship resulted in his being seduced by the jilter's charm. It was a seduction of the mind alone. Gregory saw her almost every day for two years, yet his feelings for her were given only the most rudimentary physical expression: their kissing and cuddling never inspired him to request that they continue on a more advanced scale in the bedroom. The thought, Gregory confesses, never occurred to him. Eventually, the woman did to him what she had done to his best friend – she told him, bluntly, that she had no wish to see him again.

'It was a terrible blow. I got very, very desperate. I cajoled, I even threatened. I wanted her, just a part of her, but there was no go. And then I was virtually ordered to leave. I did. On the way back home I had to pass a railway station. Something drew me to the station platform. I actually stood there, waiting for the train to come in. I was prepared to throw myself on the line, and that at the tender age of twenty-two, having survived the Palestinian horror. But fortunately something came into my mind even as the train rushed towards me, and even though it was going to be such a dramatic, theatrical effect – a voice in my head said, "She's not worth it." Those were the very words. And I stepped away from the train. It was a split-second decision.'

Gregory worked as an invoice clerk by day and studied at the City Literary Institute five evenings each week. He was conscious in his twenties of the inadequacy of his education, and was determined to correct it in some measure. He received a number of diplomas from the institute, where he took courses in English and foreign literature, history and comparative religion. He read voraciously. He was particularly interested in the writings of Freud, Adler and Jung.

He discovered the Marquis de Sade, whose work he feels has been misunderstood and continually misinterpreted.

He got 'completely dressed' for the first time when he was about twenty-eight or twenty-nine – he can't recall the exact age. His mother was out of the house and was not expected back for a few hours.

'I managed to procure a rather nice grey flannel woman's costume. I was no great shakes as a seamstress, but I managed to make it to my liking so that it fitted. I put on a corset and nylon stockings with suspenders. With the corset and a slip underneath and a blouse that I borrowed from my mother's wardrobe, and of which I took very great care, and using the right sort of towels, I managed to dress up. My mother had a pier mirror in her bedroom and I stood in front of it and stared at myself. I looked bloody scruffy, but that didn't worry me. I knew then and there that I had someone inside me who was screaming "Let me out!"'

The person who confronted him reminded him of his mother in her younger days. The wig, which he had hired from a theatrical costumier, may have had a lot to do with it: it was styled in the fashion most popular during the Edwardian era, when she was in her teens.

It was with great regret that Gregory took off the clothes that helped reveal to him his 'essential self'. He undressed slowly and reluctantly. He feared that the occasion would never occur again, that even if it did it could never be quite the same. He did not want to return to being Gregory.

He endured the unchangeable company of Gregory for a considerable time. Many years passed before he was given the opportunity to rediscover his 'essential self'. Throughout this period he was burdened with feelings of inexplicable guilt. His resulting need to be chastised caused him to seek out the prostitutes who offered strict discipline and correction. He designed a special 'punishment chair', which he constructed in the tool shed at the back of the house. He also built a pair of stocks on the instructions of a particular girl, for whom he supplied a set of ankle stocks as well.

'I wondered if I was going slightly mad. It was a compulsion; it was necessary for me to go and get punished. The

147

girls weren't at all surprised. They didn't laugh at me either. They treated me as if I were perfectly ordinary. You know that word in Greek, "catharsis" – that's exactly what it was about. I used to get it over and was very thankful really. I felt it was a clearing of my mind until the next time.'

Gregory had secured a well-paid job in the Paddington area, which meant that he had easy access to a variety of disciplinarians. One of these was Janet, who was also having problems with her personality. He was not to know how seriously disturbed she had become. Like many other prostitutes, she was an assured actress.

Cynthia's invitation to Gregory to attend one of her parties dressed as a woman marked the end of his despair. Cynthia's natural open-mindedness, her freedom from the bourgeois restraints that Gregory experienced in his relationship with his aging mother, her manner of conveying the simple message that life is to be lived as happily as possible – these were cherishable qualities to the forty-year-old man who had been forced by circumstances to smother his 'essential self'. Their friendship prospered. 'Anthea' was a respected visitor and party-goer, and Gregory a source of fascinating information – Cynthia had never encountered anyone so well-read, so knowledgeable in such a wealth of subjects, so eager to share his learning. He wrote her literally hundreds of letters, every one of which she treasures. He described his dual nature in a poem he presented to her, called *Doppel-gänger*:

> Strange entity within this flesh contained;
> Grey alter-ego of my male hardness
> Decrees me hers, and demon-sovereign like
> Bids me become her handmaiden regardless.
>
> At royal command art *cosmetique* I'll use,
> On quivering lip imprint moist Cupid bow,
> Cheeks rouge and eyes mysterious make,
> Kohl-patinated 'neath each pencilled brow.
>
> A rubbered corset fastened round my waist
> Will render figure smaller far than mine,

And over this silk knickers *directoire*
Distil in movement sensation divine.

A cheating bra will lack of bust correct
And rayon slip adorn my new physique,
Bright coloured skirt round nyloned legs will flow,
With each foot cased anew in leather sleek.

Fresh curlèd wig short hair will swiftly hide,
And gleaming necklace dangle at my throat,
Gay befrilled blouse replacing sober shirt,
And silvered ear-rings strike romantic note.

Call me not mad – Crazed puppet; Fortune's fool –
Nor felon, through her damned of mortal sins.
Since innocent of guile alone I stand,
Unknowing where 'I' cease, or siren 'She' begins.

Cynthia welcomed the 'siren' into her entourage. Gregory
at last had the freedom to transform himself into 'Anthea'.
No one sniggered when 'she' entered the room, and guests
were respectful to 'her' when, in the uniform of a nippy, 'she'
waited on them. Gregory's sole sadness – a sadness with
which he has become familiar – came with the change-back
to the self he regarded as the lesser of the two. Divesting
himself of the personality of 'Anthea' still causes him indes-
cribable anguish.

Gregory left home for ever when he was forty-two. He had
long since found his mother's company oppressive, and only
filial loyalty had made him stay with her. There were scenes
when he informed her of his decision. He was inspired to
leave because of the disinterested love he felt, and feels, for
Cynthia. He became her lodger in Edencourt Road, and he
had an upstairs room at Cranmore. He now lives alone.

Gregory joined the Beaumont Society, which tries to
further the cause of transvestism. As its publications continually stress, the majority of transvestites are heterosexual and
married. A few, like Gregory, are asexual, and even fewer are
homosexual – these last are forbidden membership, because
the founders of the society believe that passive homosexuality

is what the ignorant masses assume to be the reason why men put on clothes of the opposite sex. Most transvestites want to make love to women, and to enjoy the foreplay dressed as women themselves. Not surprisingly, it is a tiny minority who sustain physically contented relationships with their wives.

Since he was released by Cynthia, Gregory has attended various conferences for transvestites. He described how he prepares 'Anthea' for such an occasion:

The previous day you denude yourself of body hair – on the chest, on the legs, the arms and armpits. Hair is part of the masculine ethos. On the morning of the conference, you get up early and bathe very carefully. You manage to bunk yourself underneath so that your male organ is in no way discernible. Then you put on your underclothes, and some sort of foundation – I usually use bra-fillers in those places. You put on a corset and the stockings and you do it in a kind of trance, as it were. You have to learn to do these things naturally. You master the art of putting on a stocking purely by the rough expedient of having ruined a pair – masculine nails having ripped holes in them, or by being too eager to pull them up. You learn the hard way. The secret is not to hurry.

Once you've got your stockings on straight (Mitch's seams were all over the bloody shop!), you fasten them up to the suspenders and it's then that you're looking at someone in the mirror who is beginning to become feminine. The body is starting to look rounded. It's now that the feelings start for me (I can't vouch for others) – when the underslip is in place and the lingerie pinned so that the straps don't fall off your shoulders. You put a pair of slippers on your stockinged feet. You sit down at your dressing-table. You've previously shaven very, very close. You massage a little foundation cream into the beard and all the time you're concentrating on that face, which is gradually, inch by inch, changing. Now whether it's actually changing or whether it's merely changing in your imagination, I'm not prepared to say – I don't think any transvestite would say it *really* changes. We'd like to say it *really* changes, but how could it? Inside the mind it does – that's what's important. Slowly, as the face alters, a feeling comes over you – you've never known a feeling like it. The odd hair comes down, the line of the eyebrow, the curl of the eyelashes – you know the song 'I enjoy being a girl', that's how I feel. When I'm 'Anthea' a certain co-quettishness manifests itself. I'm all of a sudden impish. It's not that I want to shock people. It's just that I want to say 'This is me. I'm not Gregory, I'm not the soberly dressed man who travels on the bus to work every day, I am me.' It's at that stage that I begin to feel confident with myself.

Nevertheless, Gregory – who regards himself as a 'tender' transvestite – has not gained the confidence to travel in public as 'Anthea'. On a few occasions, 'she' has strolled down the street and bought a newspaper at a local shop. 'She' attends drag balls as well as conferences, but is always transported to them by car. Two years ago, 'Anthea' spent 'a very pleasant afternoon' wandering round the Natural History Museum. No one, it seems, 'read' Gregory – he wasn't asked to leave by a keeper, and none of the dozens of people who were there that day paid any attention whatsoever to the middle-aged lady with the Marcelle waves who was wearing a tasteful two-piece. This was a rare outing, however. The fear of being 'read', and consequently mocked, means that 'Anthea' is confined to Cranmore, where mockers have never been welcomed.

One of Cynthia's favourite partygoers is a man she refers to affectionately as Old Humphrey. This former night-watchman discovered the delights of sex when he was sixty-two. Until then, he had never even masturbated. Humphrey cannot recall ever having a wet dream: 'I've heard about them, of course. I've met blokes who've had them. But I can't say as how I remember waking up with my pyjamas in a sticky state.'

Old Humphrey looked after his elderly parents until their deaths some fourteen years ago. He now cares for his younger sister, who is mentally retarded. Much as he loved his mother and father, he experienced a sense of relief when they were gone. Having no one except his sister to wait on, Humphrey found his thoughts dwelling on the subject they should have dwelt on half a century earlier. On the verge of retirement, Humphrey endured the pangs of puberty.

Like any furtive schoolboy, Humphrey locked himself in the bathroom and eased his pleasant ache with the aid of photographs of naked women. On his way to work one evening, he picked up a discarded contact magazine on the top deck of a bus, and realized that he might have the opportunity to satisfy his longings with something more substantial than an image. He was fortunate that Cynthia was among the advertisers in that well-thumbed issue. He wrote to her, and his modestly phrased, and obviously genuine, letter earned him an invitation to Edencourt Road.

The unshockable Cynthia could not believe Humphrey when he assured her that he was a virgin. He was a masturbator, what's more, of only a few weeks' standing. It was a matter of minutes before Cynthia was convinced that the reticent old man was speaking the truth. She told him not to worry. She knew just the right person to initiate him.

That person was Mavis. A meeting was arranged between Old Humphrey and the 'bloody wonderful' French polisher. Humphrey's, therefore, was a most sophisticated initiation: nothing in his recent wild imaginings had prepared him for the marvels wrought by Mavis's lips, teeth and tongue. He had, he suddenly comprehended, a vast amount of wasted time to make up for, and he asked Mavis if she would help him fulfil his late-flowering ambition. She said she would, and she did.

Agatha aided him, too, with her usual exuberance. She took him upstairs during one of Cynthia's sex parties, and the 'poor old boy' was greeted on his descent with poached eggs on toast, which Cynthia had anticipated he would desperately need: 'She always exercised the blokes to their limits.'

Old Humphrey was one of several beneficiaries of Cynthia's special discount scheme for pensioners. He is seventy-six now. He is adamant that meeting the Streatham madam ensured him more than a decade of unexpected happiness.

Shortly before the police raid on Cranmore, Cynthia had begun to think seriously about including disabled younger men among her clients.

It is particularly galling to Cynthia that the present laws prevent her from offering what she considers a necessary service. The friendly atmosphere she assiduously created at Ambleside Avenue is ideal, she believes, for the types of customer who are too often treated by prostitutes with indifference, derision, and in many cases, total rejection. At least four of Cynthia's girls are willing to accommodate someone like Desmond, for example, who is denied the use of both legs and his left arm.

Desmond, who is in his mid-twenties, expressed his sexual frustration to his father when he was about nineteen. Mr Brown could think of only one way in which to help his son. Very much against his will, but because there was absolutely no alternative, he took Desmond to a prostitute who worked in a basement room in Earls Court. A basement *room*, not a flat. Mr Brown manœuvred his son in the wheelchair down the steps, and told the prostitute that he would call back for Desmond in an hour. Embarrassed, he left. Desmond, who was in a state of almost manic excitement, was given extremely rapid hand relief. For the next fifty minutes, he had to watch while the woman performed with three more clients – there was no possible escape for him, since the only other room was the lavatory, which was in constant use. Desmond felt acute humiliation.

Desmond's unhappy experience is not an isolated one. He paid two visits to Cranmore in 1978, and both were memorable. The party guests did not afford him special treatment, which he was quick to appreciate – they talked to him as if he were a regular Cranmorian. He did not 'go upstairs', but was wheeled into the Group Sex Room on the ground floor, which was left temporarily vacant for him and the girl of his choice. He would like to return to Cranmore in the near future.

So would Benny, an alert and witty young man who has been as much the victim of seemingly beneficial science as he has of malign nature. Benny was afflicted with Still's disease – a form of rheumatoid arthritis occurring in children – when he was three years old. He was treated with a 'wonder drug' with appalling results. His growth was impeded, so that he is now – at the age of twenty-six – under four feet tall. He has lost most of his hair. His face is that of a boy of eleven. He is partially sighted. In September 1981, he underwent a series of orthopaedic operations. It is quite likely that very soon he will be unable to walk without sticks. He may, like Desmond, have to be confined to a wheelchair.

Benny, against all the odds, is charming and amusing. He has had an affair with a girl of his own age that lasted for eighteen months. He wants to marry some day. In the meantime, he has a considerable sexual drive. When he was eighteen, he went to a sauna in Leeds, where a masseuse gave him hand relief. On a second visit, this same masseuse let him have complete intercourse with her. He talks happily of a nurse in one of the many hospitals he has stayed in who did to him in the privacy of a capacious cupboard what Beryl did, and does, to Kasper in the public arena.

Benny has been to Cranmore once. He cannot think of any experience he would prefer to repeat.

Cynthia is not blind to the discontent, amounting to open hostility, her method of running a brothel caused among professional – as distinct from occasional – prostitutes. They considered her prices insultingly low and they resented the fact that she employed women who performed both for fun and for a little extra money. When Cynthia was last in business, not more than half a dozen full-time prostitutes were working for her.

'Why do you think I've kept my clients? It's because I can guarantee them girls who will be loving on the bed. Most women on the game don't even kiss the punters, let alone do what my girls do. I don't order them to kiss, but they know I'm grateful if they do. Some prostitutes get hard, and they end up hating men's guts, and I can't say I blame them. I had a really beautiful prostitute here at a party, and she didn't go upstairs once. The men preferred Agatha to Miss Frosty-Face, who made no bloody effort to be friendly at all. I don't look for beauty in my girls – it's character I'm after. Character and honesty.'

Cynthia introduced what she calls her 'luncheon voucher system' when she was working at Edencourt Road. 'The men preferred to pay me direct. They thought it was less like a commercial transaction that way. Not having to hand over money to the girl they'd just been to bed with made it a bit more romantic for them.' Unfortunately, one or two girls who weren't regulars abused the system, and purchased vouchers from a stationer's. 'I knew they hadn't been upstairs fifteen times – they looked far too bloody fresh.' Cynthia's childhood friend, Pat, who worked for a printer's, solved the problem. She discovered a whole cache of tokens that had been printed for private distribution, and which couldn't be forged. She gave them to Cynthia, and the system was never abused again.

Cynthia maintains that men like Old Humphrey and her other old boys would not be happy visiting Soho and Earls Court, where business is strictly business. One of her longest-lasting clients is a man whose wife became paralysed when she was thirty. 'He's told her all about my establishment. He used to come here with her full permission. I should think she's worried where he goes to these days. She told him to tell me that I had saved their marriage.'

Where, Cynthia wonders, does the Knicker Man go now that Cranmore is closed to him? The Knicker Man is a solicitor in his fifties who used to visit Ambleside Avenue on brothel days. He would sit naked on the bed in the Mirror Room while a favourite girl – Jeannette, or the outrageous Rowena, who is a professional striptease artist – paraded up and down in front of him clad only in seven pairs of lace knickers. The Knicker Man enjoys pretending that he is a regimental sergeant-major. 'Halt!' he bellows, and the girl stops marching. 'First pair of knickers OFF!' he shouts. The girl removes the first pair accordingly. This process continues for roughly twenty minutes, by which time six pairs of knickers have been discarded. 'Seventh pair OFF!' he shrieks, as his frenzied right hand induces ejaculation.

Where, too, is the sweet old clergyman who, when asked by Cynthia what she could do for him, replied 'I crave an ample angel'? Pressed to elucidate, he declared that he would enjoy nothing better in this earthly life than the comfort of a buxom blonde clothed in white samite and – here he hesitated – sprouting wings. Cynthia told him she needed a little while to think it over – angels weren't that easy to come by.

Ever attentive to the demands of her clients, Cynthia persuaded a comely blonde of her acquaintance to be fitted for a long flowing cotton shift, which was run up at short notice by a dressmaker in the neighbourhood. The wings were a problem, though. They caused her worry for a week or more. Then she had another of her brainwaves. She went along to a celebrated theatrical costumier's and inquired if they possibly had a pair of wings – golden, for preference – that she could hire.

They had. The clergyman was contacted, and invited to Cranmore the following afternoon. He duly appeared, in clerical garb. Cynthia led him into the lounge, where the sight he had been longing for awaited him – posing majestically before the fireplace was the most generously bosomed of divine messengers, whispering a provocative 'Hullo'.

Cynthia left them there, but not before noticing that the vicar had started to salivate in an alarming manner. The angel, she was later informed, had been most ferociously deprived of her wings – to such an extent, indeed, that the angel had been sorely tempted to say something distinctly unangelic. Before she could utter the profanity, however, her shift was lifted and normal service was resumed. The vicar returned to his parish in a cheerful condition, and a slave was commanded by his inventive Mistress to straighten the golden wings that the old boy in his ardour had inadvertently bent.

EPILOGUE

'No horse was frightened'

By the end of April 1980, Cynthia Payne was a national
celebrity. For most people in the British Isles, the words
'luncheon vouchers' had now taken on a second meaning.
The phrase, so casually used by Cynthia during the raid, was
seized upon with delight by newspaper reporters. The occupants of the staircase at Cranmore – the eager clerics, barristers and businessmen – were portrayed by the majority of the
media, with some accuracy, as Chaucerian figures: genial old
buffers; kindly old reprobates.

Cynthia was well served by the British press – most surprisingly by those tabloids that carry titillating pictures of
naked girls on one page and high-mindedly vindictive editor-
ials about the increase of vice on another. There seemed to
be general agreement that Cynthia and her unique establishment were harming no one. Cynthia was soon given the
sobriquet 'Madam Sin', while her hitherto seemingly respectable residence became known as the 'luncheon voucher
brothel'. Naughtiness, rather than wickedness, had been on
offer in sleepy Streatham, and the nation responded to that
naughtiness with grateful laughter at a time when its political
and economic affairs were in depressing disarray.

The sixteen months between the raid and her trial at the
Inner London Crown Court were troublesome ones for Cynthia; her resilience was tested to the utmost. For one thing,

there was the uncertainty about her future: she was convinced that she would be sent to prison. More important, though, and infinitely more worrying, was the state of her health. Throughout 1979, she felt extremely weak and lethargic and was subject on occasions to unbearable pain. She consulted a specialist eventually, who diagnosed that one of her kidneys was so diseased that its removal was a matter of urgency. Her house was raided again in April of that year while a small party was in progress. Then her father died. She began to believe, as she later told a newspaper reporter, that she was a 'marked woman'.

Her kidney was removed in King's College Hospital. The doctors and staff who attended her were impressed by her cheerfulness and the positive attitude she displayed towards her operation. She entertained the nurses with stories about the brothel. She probably told them about the poor old boy who always took out his teeth before settling down to cunnilingus. Such was his excitement one evening that he snatched up a pile of tissues from the bedside table and consigned them to the toilet without realizing that they were wrapped round his dentures. 'He was lucky he was a bachelor. Just imagine if he'd had to explain why they were missing to his wife.'

Cynthia's trial took place on Monday April 21st, 1980, before Judge David West-Russell. She admitted exercising control over three prostitutes and keeping a disorderly house in December 1978. She pleaded not guilty to a further ten charges, which were not proceeded with. The prosecuting counsel, Mr Donald Farquharson, informed the court how the brothel was run and what facilities were available to its clients. 'Some of the prostitutes are described as amateurs because they were only taking part in the exercise to raise money for Christmas.' He went on to explain the luncheon voucher system, and revealed that certain pornographic films had been seized, along with items for bondage and various sex aids. Five hundred and sixty pounds in cash had been found on the premises.

The defending counsel, Mr Geoffrey Robertson, began by saying that not one of his client's neighbours had ever complained about the way in which she was using the house. The bondage equipment, which the prosecution had referred to, was not in use at the party – these items had been brought to Ambleside Avenue by individual customers for their isolated pleasure. Robertson then accounted for the clientèle, with descriptions from the police statements of the men who were seen arriving at Cranmore: 'Man in dark suit, 45–50, bald, black blazer'; 'Elderly man with trilby hat, carrying briefcase'; 'Middle-aged man, smart appearance, smoking pipe.'

Cynthia Payne, her lawyer continued, provided assistance, certain facilities, beds, and food and drink. There was no suggestion that she rounded up or recruited women. They were never obliged to have sex, and were free to say no to a customer if that was their wish. 'This was very much an informal arrangement.' The prostitutes wanted a safe house where their trade was neither difficult nor dangerous. 'They preferred to ply their trade in the security of Ambleside Avenue. But Cynthia Payne's earnings were not great. She did not live in great opulence and style.'

In his plea for leniency, Robertson spoke of the difficulties of Cynthia's early life and the circumstances in which she came to open a brothel. There was no question, he asserted, of 'beardless youngsters being initiated into the fleshpots'. The clients, who had not been touted for but mostly recommended by word of mouth, were entertained in reasonable surroundings. The men and women who used her establishment were all responsible for their own actions.

The court was shocked when Judge West-Russell sentenced Cynthia to eighteen months' imprisonment for keeping a disorderly house. She was also fined £650 for each charge of exercising control over prostitutes and ordered to pay legal costs of £2,000. The judge said that he saw no reason why the public should pay for the lengthy police time involved.

Many members of the public, including Cynthia's immediate neighbours, saw no reason why the police had gone to so much bother to raid that harmless household in the first place. Residents of Ambleside Avenue recalled how the street, which is on a bus route, was cordoned off for several hours on December 6th, 1978 – thus causing considerable traffic problems. They also wondered why quite so many policemen and policewomen had been assigned to the task of escorting fifty-three middle-aged to elderly men and seventeen women to Streatham police station for questioning. 'It was a case of overkill,' said one neighbour.

That same public expressed outrage at what Selma James of the English Collective of Prostitutes called a 'barbaric sentence'. 'The judge's colleagues were the clients,' she said. 'That was made quite clear in the court. We are not against the men getting away, but we are against the woman *not* getting away.'

Four days after the court case, the *Spectator* published an editorial which wittily and lucidly examined the precise nature of this act of legal barbarism. At one point, its writer alluded to the actress Mrs Patrick Campbell's famous observation about homosexuals: 'I don't care what they do, so long as they don't do it in the street and frighten the horses.'

The Hypocrisy of the Law

No doubt the member of the House of Lords, the Eire MP, the vicars, barristers, solicitors, accountants and businessmen who found their Christmas party in 1978 rudely interrupted by the incursion of a great number of policemen were very worried at the time. They had paid £25 each for tickets to the party in Ambleside Avenue, Streatham, and for their cash they were provided with food, drink, a dirty film, a live sex show and the opportunity of intercourse with one of the party's attendant women. Some of these women were apparently regular prostitutes, others 'amateurs' earning some extra cash for Christmas. The police duly noted the names and addresses of the men, interviewed them, then sent them on their way. They were mainly middle-aged and elderly, and had heard of the goings-on at the house in Ambleside Avenue by mailing-list and word of mouth. It was, by all accounts, the policemen's included, a well-run sort of place, as, indeed, it might be expected to be, given the quality of its clientèle. But, on account of what was going on in it, it was a disorderly house, a brothel. Mrs [sic] Cynthia Payne this week was sentenced to 18 months imprisonment, fined £1,950 and ordered to pay costs not exceeding £2,000 for keeping the house and exercising control over the prostitutes. The prosecuting counsel told the judge that there was no question of coercion or corruption of young people and that the clients 'knew perfectly well what they were doing.' None of the neighbours complained, and so far as is known, no horse was frightened.

The judge did not accept that Cynthia Payne was ignorant of the law; she had been before the courts four times previously. She had 'transgressed the law' and 'had chosen that way of life' he said, before sending her down. Her counsel pleaded that she not be jailed. She alone faced the court. 'Cynthia Payne recognises that the party is over,' he said, 'and she, and she alone, is picking up the tab. The men who flocked to Ambleside Avenue have gone free.' Indeed they have. And they have also gone unnamed. But Cynthia Payne, who catered for their tastes, is now in prison. She pleaded guilty and presumably the judge considers she has received her just deserts.

Just deserts? It is very difficult to discern any justice in this very typical case. The punishment itself is altogether excessive: nothing is gained in imprisoning Cynthia Payne and her kind unless they have corrupted the young and innocent. The transactions between Mrs Payne, her male clients and the women in her house were transactions between freely consenting adults. According to the law, the men committed no offence, and if the women did, they were not charged with any. Only Cynthia Payne is regarded as legally culpable, even though she, the men and the women were all engaged in the joint exercise of an improper Christmas party.

The law has been enforced: but justice has manifestly not been done. The quite unnecessarily severe sentence apart, there remains an outrageous indecency in the law as it stands and is enforced. If prostitution be an offence punishable at law, then a law should be written and enacted to this effect; and, if offence it be, then the man and woman, clearly sharing the offence, should be held to be both of them culpable. Commonsense would go further, and say that, of the two, the man – who, after all, is creating the demand and supplying the cash – is the more responsible for the illegal enterprise, the more culpable and the more appropriate to be punished.

But our legislators have not wished prostitution as such to be an offence, precisely in order to avoid the punishment – and the publication of the names – of the men whose demands create the supply. Not willing, however, to let the matter rest, they have sought to punish the women, and the men who control or live off the women, while leaving the demanding men alone. There are thus punishments for offences such as soliciting, living off immoral earnings, and running disorderly houses. The house in Ambleside Avenue was extremely orderly; but disorderly in law it was held to be, and Cynthia Payne goes down for 18 months.

The hypocrisy of the law as it stands could not be better illustrated. Legislators, clergymen and lawyers go unnamed and free; the woman who met their demands goes to jail. The law should be changed, so that what passes privately between consenting adults, corrupts no minors, creates no public nuisance, disturbs no neighbours and frightens no horses is no longer the concern of the law, is no longer a matter for the curiosity of the police and the prurience of the rest of us.

These views were echoed in newspapers as disparate as the *Guardian*, the *Daily Express*, the *Daily Mirror* and *The Times*. Even the prurient press concurred with most of them.

Cynthia was sent to Holloway Prison, where she witnessed lesbian displays in which the ecstasy wasn't simulated. With her customary cheerfulness, she decided to make her internment as bearable as possible: she was determined not to give in to self-pity. And anyway, she was fascinated by the women around her. She wrote to Gregory:

They have given me the job of kitchen hand (trusted job) so I will not be couped up in my dorm all day long plus the fact I may be able to get better food. There are 8 girls to a dorm, and because of shortage of staff we are shut up all day though the screws try to get us out at least once. Those days are terrible as they seem so long ... My experience of Holloway isnt a bad one, I expected terrible things to happen. I find prison officers firm but kind, some quite motherly, my favourite is a big woman who struts about like a Sgt. Major. They tell me she is genuinely concerned with the prisoners welfare. She has a great sense of fun. Another one is a tall attractive blonde with steel blue eyes. She is very strict, and would make a bomb in my house just holding a whip in her hand. The girls in my room are quite friendly to me which is a great asset because it can get miserable if they dont like you.

Some times the girls go mad at night and scream like mad at each other like monkeys because their nerves are bad. Mainly those types are unbalanced anyway. Sometimes girls cry in their sleep for their children. Others make a scene to get attention from the Officers. They have no families or friends who visit them so they feel lonely and rejected. Those types bash everything in their room. Screws take everything out so they can't hurt themselves. They give them a few hours to settle down and if they dont they have to have an injection to quieten them ... We had a lovely girl of 25 with long hair beautiful spoken had a drug problem. Nearly died with it in hospital, her one thought on release was to get another fix. She told us she had no confidence without it, and we all tried to make her see sense but it was'nt going to be any use. There is a little Vietnam woman (came on the boats) about 42, who giggles to herself in bed, and when the lot of us get bored we tend to take the 'micky' but she's good at taking a joke against herself. She's not quite normal, but is cute enough to take all her belongings and food and hide it in the bed with her so no-one goes to pinch it. Eats her food in the middle of the night ...

On Tuesday April 22nd, the first full day of Cynthia's sentence, Mitchell gave newspaper reporters a conducted tour of Cranmore. He donned a woman's wig for the occasion, and told the assembled journalists that he was a deviant. He showed them the Mirror Room, the Group Sex Room and drew their attention to a wooden plaque that hung in the kitchen: 'My house is CLEAN enough to be healthy ... and DIRTY enough to be happy'.

Cynthia's legal advisers and several old Cranmorians were annoyed with Mitchell for behaving so irresponsibly. Yet, in retrospect, Cynthia appreciates the method in the Squadron Leader's seeming madness: 'He made a joke of the whole issue. He let the world know that we had a lot of bloody wonderful fun in Ambleside Avenue.'

Cynthia appealed against her sentence. On Thursday May 15th, the appeal was heard before Lord Justice Lawton, Mr Justice Michael Davies and Mr Justice Balcombe.

In his Judgment, Lord Justice Lawton honoured those present with a short history lesson:

> The offence of keeping a disorderly house in the form of a brothel has been part of the common law in England for centuries, and from time to time it has been necessary for Parliament to intervene. The first occasion upon which Parliament did so was as long ago as in the reign of Henry III. Parliament was offended by the scandal of a number of women setting themselves up in a brothel outside the Carmelite Friary just to the south of Fleet Street.

After this preamble, His Lordship told the appellant that he and his fellow justices had decided to reduce her sentence from eighteen months' to six months' imprisonment. The fines were to be left as they were. He then stated, with the aid of 'evidence' supplied by Mr Justice Davies and the prosecuting counsel, Mr A. Wilcken, that no barristers had attended the notorious Christmas party. The two men had checked the names in the police statement with those registered in the Bar List. I am no detective, but I became suspicious when, on examining those same statements, I saw that

a Mr Lovejoy and a Mr Bedwell were questioned at Streatham station. Clearly, the barristers, along with the peer of the
realm who could not be traced in *Who's Who*, had been astute
enough, even with their pants down, to give false names and
addresses. They knew perfectly well that the police were
more concerned with charging the madam than bothering to
check their identities.

Cynthia returned to Holloway, secure in the knowledge
that if she behaved herself she would be granted remission
and released in August.

In a letter addressed to Roger, Mitchell, Gregory, Slave
Rodney, and Uncle Tom Cobleigh and all, she wrote:

> The reporters were all surprised that I stopped the car to
> allow my photo to be taken, as I could have put a coat over
> my head, but as I thought the press had been so good to
> me plus the fact that they had waited for 4 hours for a
> glimpse I thought I'd make their wait worth while. They
> all cheered when I posed for them, blowing kisses.

Cynthia was greeted outside Holloway Prison on August
20th by a client in his Rolls-Royce, Selma James with a bunch
of red roses, and a swarm of journalists. She gave her audience
the V-sign: 'V for victory, and V for voucher.'

A postcard arrived at Cranmore while Cynthia was in prison.
It was from a hopeful Mohammed, who had been told by
friends in Tangier of his former sweetheart's sudden rise to
fame. 'He probably realises now I could be a rich woman
because of it the crafty buggar,' she wrote to a relative.

For Cynthia, Cranmore is a shadow of itself these days,
particularly since Mitchell's unexpected death in the summer
of 1981. I attended his funeral and the subsequent party and
was granted a brief insight into her method of entertaining.
Her joyful cry, 'Let fucking commence!', was the cue for
decorous invitations from the gentlemen to the ladies to 'go
upstairs'. The only wildness I witnessed that day was provided by the stripper, Rowena, who performed with a dildo,

which she every so often pressed into an eager, outstretched, liver-spotted hand.

I like to believe that had Cynthia been a madam a century ago, the priggish Swinburne, who loved a lashing, would have been among her clients. This small, perky woman, with her hard-earned knowledge of the sadness and the absurdity, as well as the briefly radiant happiness, of the sexual life, is a philanthropist of sorts. She will never forget the pleasure she provided for a man who was withered from the waist down. 'I built a party around him. We had the exhibition right in front of him. After that, he chose a lovely half-caste girl. We knew he couldn't go upstairs, so all the men trooped out to the kitchen and had poached eggs on toast, and we closed the lounge doors. The girl told me afterwards that she managed to make him come. Peter, that was his name, sent me some money by post, but I wouldn't accept it. I was just so bloody overjoyed that I'd been able to give him a little happiness before he died.'

Cynthia sits in the lounge at Cranmore and longs for the freedom to give her parties again. Gregory and 'Anthea' are in attendance; Slave Philip calls twice a week to clean the house in his own special fashion, and Slave Rodney – who wept copiously the night before she entered hospital for her kidney operation – tends the garden every Saturday. And in the wings wait Agatha, Rowena, Randolph/'Tillie', the Knicker Man, Magda (who has learned, alas, that she has leukaemia), Desmond, the bank manager, Mavis, Benny, the barristers, the accountants, the clerics, the armpit-fixated diplomat, the whippers and the whipped: old Cranmorians; 'licensed jesters'; harmless people, all of them, who would be horrified to learn that they had frightened the horses.

Cynthia's mind has been active during her enforced idleness. 'I have this bloody wonderful dream. I want to widen my horizons, you see. It's my ambition to open a home for the elderly – men and women. I'd be matron. There would be special wards for the disabled. If people wanted sex, they could charge it to the National Health – the ones who can't afford it, I mean. I'd have slaves to do the cleaning and Mistresses to see that they don't cut corners. I'm surprised that no one's never thought of it before.'